A Very Basic Cooking Guide For One

Johnathan .P Felix

Introduction

This book offers a practical and informative guide for individuals who want to enjoy delicious meals while cooking for themselves. The book begins by highlighting the numerous benefits of cooking for one, including its budget-friendly nature, nutritional advantages, and the convenience it offers. It emphasizes how cooking for oneself fosters independence.

The author shares important tips for successful cooking for one, starting with the concept of "fridge-free cooking," which encourages readers to plan meals ahead and minimize food waste. The book stresses the importance of buying the right quantities and types of ingredients, making cooking an enjoyable activity, and exploring recipes that can serve as complete meals.

One valuable strategy presented is cooking a protein source once a week, which allows for easy meal preparation throughout the week. The book also suggests stocking up on essential pantry items to simplify the cooking process.

The cookbook is divided into various sections, each offering a diverse range of recipes tailored for one person. It covers all aspects of daily meals, including fast and easy breakfast ideas, lunchbox-ready lunch recipes, classic and delectable dinner recipes, with a special focus on lamb dishes. Additionally, it includes scrumptious and healthy snack and dessert recipes.

The book recognizes the importance of convenience and offers simple slow-cooking recipes, easy leftover recipes, and quick 15-minute recipes for one. For those looking for nutritious and refreshing options, there are sections dedicated to smoothies and drinks for one, as well as salads and simmering soup recipes.

Moreover, the book introduces the concept of mason jar meals, which are not only practical but also visually appealing.

Overall, this book is a comprehensive resource that addresses the unique challenges and advantages of cooking for a single person. It provides a wide array of recipes and valuable tips to inspire and empower individuals to create delicious and satisfying meals for themselves.

Contents

Chapter 1 – Benefits of Cooking for One

You are probably wondering why you should cook for one when you can easily go to any restaurant outside and eat whatever you like. It is more convenient and maybe cheaper if you consider the amount of leftovers that spoil and go to waste when you cook a lot more than you intended for yourself. You are probably thinking why bother when you do not have a family to cook for. You only have yourself to please and you are happy and satisfied eating out or ordering takeout. This feeling is especially common on a weekday, when you arrive from work depleted and tired from working eight hours or so and you just do not have the right energy and motivation to prepare the ingredients and cook a full meal. You also have the same feeling in the morning, when you feel more like sleeping another thirty minutes or so than whipping up a healthy breakfast for one. The question that you keep asking yourself is "why bother?"

The problem here is that you do not have the right motivation to cook for yourself. If you have the right motivation, it will be easier for you to make the extra effort. This is why it is important to understand the different benefits of cooking for one. Some of the most important benefits are listed in the paragraphs below.

More budget-friendly

Cooking for one is more budget-friendly than eating out and ordering takeout. When you eat out or have food delivered to your home, you are paying not only for the food but also for the service, the brand, and many other things required for producing that food. If you decide to cook your own food, you can prepare meals and buy ingredients that are within your budget. And you can still use some of the ingredients that you buy to cook one meal for other meals that you are planning to cook for the next several days. For example, if you buy a bottle of olive oil, you can use the remaining olive oil to cook other future meals. After all, you are not going to use the whole bottle for just one meal. Another reason why cooking for one is more budget-friendly is the fact that you will have no leftovers. And even if you have leftovers by cooking meals in bulk using a slow cooker and freezing the leftovers, you are saving even more money because you now have food for several days without buying any more ingredients.

More nutritious

Home-cooked meals are definitely more nutritious than takeouts and fast food. These are the kinds of food that you will most likely eat because these are the most convenient. However, these foods do not exactly give you the right nutrients that your body needs. These restaurants do not exactly think about the nutrient requirements of their customers. They only think about food that people will find delicious, even if it will give them a heart attack or diabetes. If you decide to cook for yourself, you can at least ensure that the food that you eat and the ingredients that you use are good for your health and overall wellbeing. You can choose not to use ingredients that are chemical-based, preservatives, artificial flavouring, and other unhealthy and artificial ingredients that you can usually find in ready-to-cook meals and fast food. If you have a special health condition, like diabetes or heart disease, you can at least prepare and cook meals that will improve your condition, or at least not make it worse. If you are on a diet to get slim, you can prepare meals that will not make you gain more weight because you can determine the amount of calories of the meals that you are planning to cook.

More convenient

Many people would say that cooking food for one is a lot of trouble than it's worth because they are only cooking for themselves. They do not have a family to prepare food for or any other member of the household who can at least be the reason why they need to spend an hour or so preparing all the ingredients and cooking the food on the stove or in the oven. If cooking for one is inconvenient, you are probably doing it wrong. Although it is great to always eat freshly cooked meals, you can also stock up on food by freezing or canning so that you will have food to reheat in those times when you are too busy to prepare a freshly cooked meal. For example, you can cook a large batch of soup which you can freeze in muffin trays so that you will have something to reheat when you have no time to whip up breakfast or when you are too tired to cook dinner. You can cook this using a slow cooker where all you need to do is toss all the ingredients and let the slow cooker do the cooking. You can do other things while it is cooking, like clean the house, run errands, go to work, and so on.

Makes you more independent

One of the reasons why people do not want to cook for themselves is because they do not know how to cook. They have been living with their parents for many years and this is the first time that they will live by themselves with no one to cook for them. They always end up eating outside or ordering takeout because they have no idea how to cook. If this is your reason, when will you learn if not now? If you know how to cook for yourself, you will be more independent. You can live anywhere and be able to eat good food because you know how to cook for yourself. And if you are single and decide to get married sometime in the future, knowing how to cook is a great advantage whether you are a man or woman because you and your partner can take turns preparing nutritious meals for your whole family. If you have guests, you can impress them with your cooking skills by learning how to cook for yourself first. This is something that you will be grateful for as you grow older and eating pizza and burgers just no longer interests you.

Aside from keeping yourself motivated with all these benefits of learning how to cook for one, you also need to do other strategies that will encourage you to cook for one such as the ones listed below.

- *Eat afternoon snacks.* Some people are too hungry to cook dinner and often end up calling their favourite fast food and ordering pizza or anything that does not require cooking. They no longer have energy to prepare and cook food because they do not have any energy left after working hard for several hours straight. This is why it is advisable to eat afternoon snacks before you leave work so that you will not feel too hungry before dinner. You can grab an apple or a protein bar just to keep your sugar levels stable until dinner. This will encourage you to cook dinner even if you are just cooking for yourself.

- *Try to cook delicious meals for one.* Another reason to get more motivated to cook for your own self is to cook something that will make your mouth water. The last few chapters of this book are dedicated to easy and delicious recipes for one. You can try some of these that will encourage you to prepare you own food at home. There are many things that you can do to prepare nutritious food for yourself and through the course of this book you will learn exactly how to do so.

- *Be more conscious in making decisions.* Before you give in and dial your local fast food to order pizza or something, you should first ask yourself if it really what you want to do. Are you really that tired that you cannot cook dinner for yourself, which will only take you less than an hour? Think about all the benefits of cooking for your own self. More often than not, people give in to their hunger pangs or current mood which is why they often end up not bothering to cook at all, when in fact, eating home-cooked dinner is something that they really want.

- ❖ ***Cook foods that are easy to store.*** So make pastas and curries that can be easily boxed up and stored in the freezer. Don't make extremely elaborate meals that will turn out to be a headache for you. Plan it out in such a way that you only use a few ingredients and make dishes that are easy to make and easier to store.

Chapter 2 - Important "Cooking for One" Tips

You got this book for a reason: you are tired of microwave TV dinners, canned food and unhealthy takeouts. You want to enjoy fast, delicious, cheap and healthy meals that will make eating alone a worthwhile experience. Well, good news, for this book will guide you through the journey of healthier eating!

From now on, your kitchen will be your best friend. If there is something about your kitchen that you don't like (such as the paint on the walls) then go ahead and change it. You will be spending a bit more time in this part of your home so why not make it a fun experience every time.

One big advantage of cooking for one is that dish washing won't be such a chore. All you will ever need is one pair of cutlery, one bowl, one plate, one cup and one glass. And just because you're cooking for one does not make it a rush all of the time. Dedicate a table and a chair to be your dining area, spread an attractive tablecloth over it and place a vase with some fresh cut flowers in it. Create a playlist to serve as your background music while you are eating to set the right ambiance. Hang a lantern over a light bulb to set the mood for eating at home.

The dining experience aside, you will want to have the sharpest equipment at hand in your kitchen in order to prepare your meals.

What You'll Need in a Kitchen for One

You won't be required to purchase kitchen equipment suitable for a chef. In fact, this book is especially written with people from small apartments and dormitories in mind. Let's go by the principle of working with what you have; only buy additional kitchen equipment if you have set aside a specific budget for it.

Here is a list of necessary items in your kitchen, enumerated based on importance:

- **A sharp knife.** If there is one necessary tool in your kitchen, then it should be this. You will need it in most recipes, from slicing meat to chopping vegetables.

- **Two bowls, a large one and a small one.** The smaller bowl is where you will be eating most of your meals from, while the larger bowl will make salad tossing an easier affair.

- **A nonstick frying pan and spatula.** Using nonstick will make it a breeze to wash and will spare you from using oil while cooking.

- **Hot plate.** This will make cooking for one a lot cheaper compared to using a stove top. That's because it can be used anywhere no matter how small your living space may be.

- **A small rice cooker.** This nifty little appliance will stretch beyond plain old rice and let you cook a wide array of dishes.

- **A toaster oven.** It is far more practical to use this for broiling and baking because it does not take long to heat up.

- **A personal refrigerator.** This is the last on the list because it is quite a luxury. However, if you can afford it then it truly is a worthwhile investment.

Make sure that all of these are placed in the same place like your island's drawers. You have to access them fast enough and get cooking at the earliest, lest you feel lazy and decide to call for food!

Fridge-free Cooking

In case you don't have a refrigerator yet, you will not be able to stockpile on any ingredients that would require it. Thankfully, many grocery stores offer individual or travel-sized servings. Even if they are not as cheap as bulk, you will still end up saving more money compared to them getting spoiled. Locate the nearest grocery store that offers individual servings in your daily route or near your home.

In the meantime, you can keep your food items in a cooler that is packed with ice. Just ensure that you've got the food sealed tightly in containers since the ice will still continue to melt.

Plan your Meals Ahead

The secret to successfully staying within your budget and enjoying delicious one serving meals at the same time is through planning. Set aside an hour each week and dedicate it to planning your breakfast, lunch and dinner meals.

A meal plan will serve as your guide for purchasing the right ingredients since you will know exactly what to do with them once you get home. Even eating out and takeouts can be included in your plan, especially during days when you simply do not have energy left to prepare a dish yourself.

Also, you can cook in bulk and divide the servings into separate containers which you can simply grab and heat up during mealtimes. This method will certainly save you a lot of money and time in the long run.

Recycle leftovers

It is always a good idea to recycle your left overs. When you do so, you end up with a ready meal which can be assembled in no time at all. All you have to do is add it to a pan and add in some seasoning. Your meal will be ready and you can consume it instantly! Food will remain good in the fridge for up to 2 days and you can mix and match different foods to come up with a dish. For example: if you have left over rice and chicken salad then you can toss them together along with soya sauce, chilies and salt to make a quick fried rice. So it's up to you to mix and match and make the most of all your left overs.

Fresh dinners

Although recycling leftovers is always a good idea, it is not the best idea. So it will be great if you can cook fresh dinner every night and not settle for the same thing night after night as it can get monotonous. Look for unique recipes and use them every day. You will experiment a bit at the beginning but then you will get accustomed to a few go to dishes that you will prepare within no time.

Freezer

When you are cooking solo meals, the freezer will be your best friend! You will have to prepare meals and fill it up in plastic cups. Then you stick it into the freezer and remove and reheat it before consuming it. This will ensure that the food remains fresh for a long time and you can eat it over a few days.

Chapter 3 – More "Cooking for One" Tips

Aside from the essential "cooking for one" tips that you have learned in the previous chapter, you need to learn more tips and tricks that will make cooking for one a lot easier and more convenient. You already have an idea what kind of kitchen gadgets you need to have in your kitchen and some tips for preparing fridge-free meals and planning your meals ahead. Here are some more tips that will make your cooking for one experience hassle-free.

Buy the right amount

There are two ways to shop for cooking ingredients—one is to buy them in bulk and the other is to buy them in single serving packages. If you are planning to cook in bulk using a slow cooker, you can buy food items in bulk like grains, beans, and sugar. If you do not want to have any leftovers, you can buy food items in single serving such as cheeses in individual wraps, eggs, canned goods, microwaveable bacon, and single-serve condiments that you can use in one meal without any leftovers. You should only buy the single-serve food items if you are really going to use them once and if they do not have a long shelf life. It is ideal to buy in bulk if the item lasts for a long time in storage, like sugar, flour, beans, or grains. For fresh produce like fruits and vegetables, it is best to buy them in pieces rather than in bags. You do not want to have a bunch of rotten fruits and vegetables in your kitchen after a few days. When you hit the super market, go to the bulk sell department and buy everything that you need in bulk. You can then stock it up in your house or kitchen. It is always a good idea to be extreme couponers. You can look for appropriate coupons in the paper and online and use it to buy food from the supermarket. You will have the chance to save on a lot of money by doing so. Look for a departmental store near your house that takes these coupons in bulk and gives you a heavy discount.

Buy the right kind

People who are living alone usually end up buying a lot of ready-to-eat meals or instant food. There is really nothing wrong with eating these but make sure that you don't do it frequently. These ready-to-eat and instant meals are not good for your health if you consume them on a daily basis. Stay away from the aisle with lots of instant and no-cook food and instead go to the produce section where you will find a lot of fresh food. This is easy to do because most pre-packaged meals and instant food are in the center aisles while fresh produce are along the edges of the grocery. You should also consider befriending your local fishmonger or butcher so that you can buy meat and fish in small pieces.

It is also important to stock up on common ingredients that you can use in different meals. Do not buy a lot more of those exotic ingredients than you need in your recipe because you might end up with a lot of it left in your pantry because you have no idea how to use them in other meals. You should buy pasta, grains, canned or frozen meats and fish, sauces, salad dressings, fresh produce, cheeses, and eggs.

Make cooking fun

You can make cooking more fun by doing something different aside from chopping vegetables, slicing meat and fish, boiling pasta or grains, and washing dishes. You can listen to music and sing your favorite songs. You can also drink a bottle of wine and turn it into a special weekly occasion, especially if you don't get to do it every day. You can invite a friend over so that you can cook not only for one but for two people. You can read a book while waiting for something to boil or you can turn on the TV and watch a movie or

TV series. Just make sure that you do not get too engrossed in what you are doing or you might end up with a burnt meal for one.

Cook for more than one person

This may seem contradictory to this whole book but cooking for more than one person is actually a sound advice for people who live alone. Cooking for every meal may require a lot more effort and time than cooking for more than one person if you are living by yourself. If you cook a large batch of, say, soup or chilli, you can always freeze the rest of the food for future use. Just make sure that you have a deep freezer that allows you to store already cooked foods for weeks. You need to label the food that you store in the freezer. Write the date when the food was cooked and the contents on the container or packaging. When properly frozen most cooked foods will keep within one to three months. You can also cook food for two or three people and keep the leftovers in the fridge, if you have one. You can just pop the leftovers in the microwave for reheating or use them as an ingredient for a whole new different dish. There is a separate chapter for cooking leftovers to you might want to check it out.

Choose recipes that can be a complete meal

Cooking a separate main dish and a separate side dish can be a bit of a hassle especially if you have a small kitchen with limited cooking utensils and very limited time. What you can do is to cook a dish that can serve as your whole meal. Find "cooking for one" recipes that have the main food groups like protein, carbohydrates, fats, and vitamins, and other minerals. Some examples of such recipes are chicken casserole, vegetarian chilli, vegetable or beef stew, and so on. These recipes are best prepared in slow cookers where all you need to do is toss all the ingredients in the pot and wait for it to cook. These complete meals will also make for great office carry meals as you wont have to pack things separately. Buy yourself a large tiffin carrier and carry your own meals to office! This will help you remain motivated and will also inspire others around you. The temptation to consume foods that are not home made will reduce and you will have the chance to lead a healthy life. You can also tell people in your office to bring nutritious food from home and you can have pot luck every day of the week!

Cook your protein source once a week

Most protein sources take a long time to cook like pork, beef, chicken, turkey, and so on. You can cook these protein sources in advance in a slow cooker to save you time. For example, you slow cook turkey breast or roast a chicken over the weekend and use it as ingredients to different dishes for the rest of the week. You can add the meat to your sandwich, salad, soup, stew, tacos, burritos, and pasta. This way, you do not need to cook meat whenever the recipe calls for meat.

Stock up on cupboard essentials

You need to stock up on these following cupboard essentials that you can use for cooking for one. This will prevent you from ordering takeout or eating out and will make it easier for you to prepare food for yourself.

- *Herbs and spices.* If you want your meals to have different flavours without adding artificial flavouring or using unhealthy methods of cooking to add more flavour like deep frying, you can always use fresh or dried herbs and spices. Some examples of herbs and spices are thyme, cumin, paprika, oregano, basil, garlic powder, cayenne pepper, black pepper, curry powder, and cinnamon. You can easily buy these from any grocery store or you can pick fresh herbs from your own her garden. Just buy a few pots and place them in your garden and pick them fresh every day.

- **Sauces.** You should also include sauces in your grocery shopping list such as mustard, salad dressing, hot sauce, marinara, pesto, salsa, soy sauce, and mayonnaise. Always choose reduced sodium or fat when buying sauces and dressings.

- **Vinegars and oils.** You will need different kinds of oils such as olive oil, vegetable oil, sesame oil, and coconut oil. You will also need different kinds of vinegars like balsamic, red wine, and white wine.

- **Baking products.** This includes brown sugar, cornstarch, all-purpose flour, and honey. You can buy them in bulk and store them in a separate container meant exclusively for baking products.

- **Nuts, seeds, and dried fruits.** These can be added to some meals especially breakfast but can also be eaten as snacks. Some examples are dates, dried apricots, walnuts, raisins, pecans, sesame seeds, almonds, and cranberries. You can also store these in small containers and consume them as snacks.

- **Cans and packets.** You can also add canned tomatoes, beans (chickpeas, kidney, black beans, etc.), canned tuna in water, tomato paste, broth or bouillon cubes (reduced sodium), pasta, and grains.

- **Frozen food.** If you have a fridge, you need to buy frozen vegetables in bags such as spinach, mixed vegetables, and peas. You should also buy frozen fruits. If you don't buy them frozen then it is easy to freeze them. All you need is a few freezer bags and your vegetables. Some people like to use the vacuum machine to remove the air from the bag and then place it in the fridge but that is not really necessary.

- **Perishables.** You should also stock up on perishables if you have a fridge. You can store fresh onions and garlic that can last for at least a month when refrigerates, fresh fruits and vegetables, fresh meat, and dairy.

Remember that you need to season your dishes well if you wish to keep it interesting for yourself. You can also place some seasoning on the table if you like.

Cooking using non-traditional kitchen equipment

As what has been suggested in the previous chapter, you can cook even if you do not have any fridge, although of course it is much better if you have a fridge. You can also cook using other kitchen equipment aside from the stove and traditional oven. If you are creative and resourceful enough, you can whip up a delicious meal using only your toaster oven, hot plate, or rice cooker. You can broil or bake food using your toaster oven. You can roast vegetables and toast bread and sandwiches in this versatile kitchen equipment. It is perfect for your small kitchen and for your single meals because of the small size. Instead of a full size stove top, you can cook your meals using a hot plate. This is a cheap alternative that is ideal in small spaces like apartments or dorm rooms. You can cook just about anything you can cook on a real stove on your hot plate. You may think that rice cookers can only cook rice but you are wrong because it can cook delicious pot dishes like soup and stew.

Pressure cooker

I decided to explain the uses of a pressure cooker here as I think it deserves a separate section. Pressure cookers are quite common in Asian countries but not so common in the western world.

Science behind it

Now you may wonder as to how a pressure cooker works and what mechanism guides it. Well, a pressure cooker is nothing but a vessel that helps trap in pressure. The cooker is filled with food and water and then tightly sealed in such that the water starts to boil and creates a pressure inside. This pressure is then let out by placing a weight or a whistle on top. So every time there is immense pressure, the weight or whistle blows owing to steam from inside escaping. This extreme boiling causes the food inside to cook and your dish will be ready in no time. Right from pulses to grains to meat, everything is cooked in a pressure cooker as it is extremely easy to operate. You can make one pot dishes using the cooker and once the weight blows out 3to 5 times, your dish will be ready to serve.

By making use of one, you can avail several benefits, which are explained as under.

- The food that you cook will retain almost all of the nutrition and this is not possible with regular cooking methods. When you cook something in a cooker, the moisture present inside the vegetables and meat heats up and cook them. This will help you retain the nutrition and none of it will be lost.

- You can save on a lot of time by cooking in a pressure cooker. Once the water heats up, which can take 5 to 10 minutes, the steam starts to escape. At this point when you place the weight, the food begins to cook. So from start to finish, it will not take any more than 20 to 30 minutes to cook food.

- It easier to clean as all you have to clean is the vessel and lid of the cooker! You don't have to clean any messy dishes and you can be done within 5 minutes!

- You can save a lot of energy as you don't have to cut anything finely while using the cooker. Everything will turn so soft that it won't matter what size they were when they went in. even if they are really big, like big slices of potatoes, they will go mushy in no time.

- Believe it or not, your kitchen heats up just so much during regular cooking that your entire house warms up! But with the pressure cooker, your kitchen will remain cool and so will your house!

These form just some of the advantages of using pressure cookers but it is not limited to just these. Once you start using it, you will realize how useful and effective it really is!

<u>Choosing a cooker</u>

To choose a cooker, look for good quality ones that come with warranties and are quality checked. There are some good brands in the market, which you can research and buy. Most of these cookers are made of steel as it conducts heat quite fast. But you can also settle for traditional aluminum cookers that help you cook all varieties of foods. You have to be careful though, while washing your pressure cooker and make sure there are no scratches formed inside it. The rubber that is supplied with your cooker should be stretched a little before placing it inside the grooves of the lid so that it heats up the cooker faster. Many times, you will find that food has caught at the bottom. But this only happens if you don't use enough water and are cooking directly in it as opposed to using vessels. A standard pressure cooker will cost you between $30 and $100 depending on the size and capacity.

The following chapters will provide you with some simple and easy recipes for one person that you can try in your apartment or dorm room.

Chapter 4 - Fast and Easy Breakfast Recipes

Singles are usually out and about, which means preparing breakfast at home should beat purchasing expensive coffee and waffles from a cafe. Here are 6 fast and easy breakfast recipes that you can whip up within 5 to 20 minutes. Pair any one of these meals with a cup of hot coffee or a glass of orange juice.

Rice Cereal

Prep Time: 10 to 15 minutes.

Ingredients:

- 1 cup cooked rice (leftover rice is fine, just heat it up if you put it in the fridge)
- 1/4 cup milk (dairy or nut-based)
- 1 Tbsp. of finely chopped nuts (almonds, pecans, hazelnuts, etc)
- A piece of fresh or dried fruit (the ones in season are the cheapest)
- A generous dash of allspice, nutmeg and/or cinnamon
- Salt (a small pinch)
- Honey, agave or maple syrup (as much as you like)

Instructions:

1. In a nonstick pan, mash up your rice with your fork until it becomes mushy.
2. Pour in the milk and place over low heat for about 5 to 10 minutes. In the meantime, chop up your piece of fruit and

then add that to the mixture.

3. Lightly toast the chopped nuts.

4. Remove the rice cereal from the pan and into your bowl. Sprinkle the nuts on top and then drizzle your honey, agave or maple syrup on top. Enjoy!

An American Breakfast

Prep Time: 10 to 15 minutes

Ingredients:

- 1 egg
- 1 strip of fresh bacon (unseasoned and unprocessed)
- 1 or 2 slices of whole grain bread
- Optional: a sliver of margarine or butter (for your toast)
- Salt and Pepper

Instructions:

1. Heat up your nonstick pan over low-medium.

2. Cut your bacon into bite-sized pieces. Season with salt and pepper.

3. Place them on the pan and turn the heat up to medium. Let each side cook for 5 minutes.

4. Pop your bread into your toaster for 2 minutes.

5. Two minutes after turning the pieces of bacon, move them to the side and crack your egg open in the same pan.

6. Season your egg with a bit of salt and pepper. Tip the pan a bit to let its runny whites pour to its edges and become cooked.

7. Remove the egg and bacon from pan and transfer onto plate. Place toast on the side. Enjoy!

French Toast

Prep Time: 5 to 10 minutes

Ingredients:

- 2 or 3 slices of bread
- 1 egg
- 1/4 cup of milk (dairy or nut-based)
- 1 tsp of butter or oil
- Vanilla
- Salt
- Jam, butter, syrup or applesauce

Instructions:

1. In a small bowl, crack the egg and add salt and vanilla. Beat until foamy.
2. Soak the slices of bread in the egg mixture for as long as you can.
3. Heat a nonstick pan over medium and melt the butter or drizzle the oil on top.
4. Place the soaked bread in the pan and cook well. Flip once the underside is golden brown.
5. Once both sides are golden brown, remove from pan and serve on plate with a side of jam, butter, syrup or applesauce. Enjoy!

Breakfast Burrito

Prep Time: 5 to 10 minutes

Ingredients:

- 1 or 2 eggs
- 1 tortilla or pita

- 1/4 cup chopped spinach or any other greens of choice
- 2 or 3 slices of any type of cheese
- Salt and pepper
- Optional: 1 fresh tomato (diced) and salsa

Instructions:

1. Place a nonstick pan over low-medium heat and heat up the greens and diced tomato. Add a dash of salt and pepper.
2. Set veggies aside and cook the egg on the same pan (you can choose to do scrambled or sunny side up).
3. Place the cheese on top of the egg to melt it a bit.
4. Put all of the ingredients inside your tortilla or pita. Add salsa if desired. Enjoy!

Ham and Cheese Omelet

Prep Time: 5 to 10 minutes

Ingredients:

- 1 slice of ham (from the deli)
- 1 to 2 eggs
- Handful of cheese (Feta, Parmesan, Prosciutto, etc)
- Salt and pepper
- Optional: 1 small onion, sliced thinly
- Drizzle of oil (preferably olive or coconut)

Instructions:

1. Dice the ham.
2. Beat the eggs in a shallow bowl and add a dash of salt and pepper before beating it again until foamy.

3. Heat up a nonstick pan over low-medium. Once it starts to get hot, add some oil.

4. Heat up your diced ham. Transfer to a plate and set aside.

5. Sautee your sliced onion. Gradually pour in the beaten eggs. Keep adding until the underside is almost completely cooked.

6. Tilt the pan slightly to allow the runny egg mixture to fall directly on the surface of the pan and become cooked.

7. Place your ham at the center, followed by the cheese. Carefully fold the omelet. If it gets messed up, it's alright for it will still be delicious.

8. Transfer the omelet to a plate and cut across the center to let steam out. Enjoy!

Instant Muesli

Prep Time: 3 minutes

Ingredients:

- 1/4 cup nuts and seeds (a mixture of your favorites, such as walnuts, sunflower seeds, almonds, etc.)
- 1/2 cup rolled oats
- A piece of fresh or dried fruit
- Milk (dairy or nut-based)
- Optional: honey and 1 Tbsp of ground flax seeds

Instructions:

1. Slice up the fruit.
2. Combine all of the dry ingredients in your bowl.
3. Pour in the milk and let the ingredients soak it up to soften. Enjoy!

Potato Skillet

Prep Time: 10 minutes

Ingredients:

- 1 potato, peeled, diced
- 2 slices bacon
- A pinch seasoning salt
- Black pepper powder to taste
- A large pinch garlic salt
- 2 small eggs, beaten
- 2 tablespoons cheddar cheese, grated

Instructions:

1. Place a skillet over medium high heat. Add bacon and cook until crisp. Remove with a slotted spoon and keep the bacon aside.
2. To the same skillet, add potatoes, garlic salt, seasoning salt and pepper powder.
3. Cover and cook until soft.
4. Crumble bacon and add to the skillet. Pour beaten eggs over the potatoes and cook until eggs are set.
5. Sprinkle cheese all over. Cover and cook until cheese is melted.

Spinach & Mushroom Omelet

Prep Time: 15 minutes

Ingredients:

- 1 small egg

- 2 egg whites
- 1/4 cup fresh tomatoes, chopped
- 2 tablespoons green onions, chopped
- 1/4 cup mushrooms, sliced
- 1/2 cup fresh spinach, chopped
- 1 tablespoon red bell pepper, sliced
- 1/8 teaspoon salt
- A large pinch black pepper powder
- 1/2 tablespoon parmesan cheese, grated
- 1/2 tablespoon low fat cheddar cheese, grated
- A pinch red chili flakes
- A pinch ground nutmeg
- 1 teaspoon olive oil

Instructions:

1. Whisk together egg and egg whites. Add the cheese, salt, pepper, garlic powder, red pepper flakes and nutmeg. Whisk until well combined.
2. Place a nonstick pan over medium heat. Add oil. When oil is hot, add mushrooms, green onions and bell pepper. Sauté until the vegetables are tender.
3. Add spinach and sauté until spinach wilts. Mix in the tomatoes.
4. Pour egg mixture and cook until eggs are set.
5. Serve immediately.

Ricotta and Tomato toast

Prep Time: 5 minutes

Ingredients:

- 2 thick slices whole wheat bread
- 4 large tomato slices
- 1 teaspoon olive oil
- Salt to taste
- Pepper powder to taste
- 2 tablespoons part skim ricotta cheese
- 1 teaspoon fresh basil leaves, minced

Instructions:

1. Lightly toast the bread slices.
2. Spread ricotta cheese all over the bread slices.
3. Lay the tomato slices. Sprinkle oil, salt and pepper.
4. Serve immediately.

Tofu Scramble:

Prep Time: 15 minutes

Ingredients:

- 7 ounce block extra firm tofu (keep it pressed for 15 minutes to remove excess moisture), crumbled
- 1/4 cup packed kale, chopped (remove ribs)
- 1/4 cup bell pepper, seeded, diced (yellow or orange)
- 1/4 cup tomatoes, diced
- 1/4 cup green onions, diced
- 1 tablespoon nutritional yeast
- 1/8 teaspoon onion powder
- 1/8 teaspoon garlic powder

- 1/8 teaspoon turmeric powder
- 2 tablespoons avocado, diced
- 1/2 teaspoon olive oil
- Salt to taste
- Pepper powder to taste

Instructions:

1. Place a nonstick pan over medium heat. Add oil. When oil is hot, add bell pepper, green onions and kale. Sauté for a couple of minutes until the kale is wilts slightly.
2. Add turmeric and sauté for a few seconds. Add rest of the ingredients except avocado and cook for a couple of minutes.
3. Add avocado and heat thoroughly.
4. Serve it as it is or with tortillas.

Cheese Soufflé

Prep Time: 15 minutes

Ingredients:

- 1 egg, separated
- 1 tablespoon butter
- 1 tablespoon all purpose flour
- 1/4 cup cheddar cheese, shredded
- 1/4 cup milk
- A pinch salt
- A pinch pepper powder

Instructions:

1. Place a saucepan over medium heat. Add butter. When butter melts, add flour and sauté for a few seconds.
2. Slowly add milk stirring constantly and cook until thickened.
3. Lower heat and add cheese.
4. Remove from heat.
5. Beat the yolk. Add a little of the hot mixture to the beaten yolk. Add it back to the pan.
6. Stir constantly for a while. Let it cool a little.
7. Meanwhile beat the egg white until stiff peaks are formed. Gently fold it into the yolk mixture.
8. Transfer into a ramekin.
9. Bake in a preheated oven at 350 degree F for about 25 minutes or until set.
10. Serve immediately.

Breakfast Medley

Prep Time: 15 minutes + chilling time

Instructions:

- 3 tablespoons juice of your choice
- A large pinch cinnamon powder
- 1/4 cup fruits of your choice, chopped
- 1/2 tablespoon nuts, roasted, crushed
- 2 tablespoons flavored yogurt
- 1/2 tablespoon raisins
- Honey to taste

Instructions:

1. Place oats and juice in a microwavable bowl. Microwave on high for about 2 minutes. If the oats are not cooked, add some more juice and microwave for a few seconds more.
2. Transfer into a glass.
3. Layer it with rest of the ingredients in any manner you like.
4. Drizzle some more honey on top and chill for 3-4 hours before serving.

Chapter 5 - Lunchbox-Ready Lunch Recipes

Lunchtime is usually crunch time, especially for busy singles. However, that is no excuse to always grab an unhealthy lunch that will cause a wide range of illnesses in the long run. Instead, treat yourself to these 5 healthy and delicious lunch recipes that you can easily take with you to work or school.

If you have a lunch buddy who also cooks for one, you can talk to them about preparing lunches for each other. For instance, you will be the one to prepare lunch on Mondays, him/her on Tuesdays, and so on. This is a great way to save on prep time and your budget. Simply double the measurements in the ingredients to make two servings.

Stuffed Bagel Sandwiches

Prep Time: 5 minutes

Ingredients:

- 1 medium bagel
- 3 tablespoons whipped cream cheese
- 1 large slice salami, diced
- 1 1/2 tablespoons dill relish
- 3 baby carrots, chopped
- A pinch garlic powder
- A pinch salt
- A pinch pepper powder

Instructions:

1. Cut the bagel horizontally in the middle. Remove a little soft part of the bread on both the parts so that you can stuff the filling.
2. Mix together salami, salt, pepper, dill relish, carrots, garlic powder, and cream cheese in a bowl
3. Fill this mixture in one half of the cavity of the bagel. Cover with the other half.
4. Cut into 2 halves vertically. You get 2 semi circular sandwiches.
5. Wrap it in foil and pack in your lunch box.

Walnut Scones

Prep Time: 15 minutes

Ingredients:

- 1 cup self raising flour + extra for dusting
- 1/2 teaspoon baking powder
- A pinch salt
- 25 grams butter, cubed
- 1 small egg, beaten
- 1/3 cup milk
- 25 grams walnuts, chopped
- Soft goat's cheese to serve
- Jam of your choice to serve (optional)
- A few walnut halves

Instructions:

1. Mix together in a large bowl, flour, baking powder and salt.

2. Add butter. Using your fingertips, mix together the ingredients until it attains a crumbly texture. Add walnuts and mix again.

3. Add milk and form into a dough. Do not knead too much.

4. Flatten the dough into a round of 3 cm thick. Cut into wedges.

5. Place on a lined baking sheet. Brush the top of each wedge with beaten egg.

6. Place a walnut halve on each of the wedges.

7. Bake in a preheated oven at 425 degree F for about 15 minutes or until golden. It will puff up.

8. Remove from the oven and transfer on to a wire rack. Topping is optional.

9. Pack in an airtight lunch box.

Chicken and Vegetable Sautéed Rice

Prep Time: 20 minutes

Ingredients:

- 1 cup rice
- 1 1/2 cups water
- 1/2 cup chicken pieces, boneless, skinless, blanched, shredded
- 1/4 cup frozen sweet corn kernels
- 1 teaspoon garlic and ginger paste
- 1 egg, scrambled
- 1/4 teaspoon salt or to taste
- 1/8 teaspoon pepper powder
- 1 tablespoon soy sauce

- 1 chicken bouillon cube (optional)
- 2 green onions, sliced
- 1 small bell pepper, chopped
- 1/4 cup frozen green peas
- 1/4 cup snap peas
- 1/2 cup cabbage
- 1 stick celery, chopped
- 1 small carrot, chopped
- 1/8 teaspoon ajinomoto (optional)
- 2 tablespoons butter

Instructions:

1. Add water and rice to a large saucepan and cook the rice. When done, fluff with a fork.

2. Place a wok over medium heat. Add 1/2-tablespoon butter. When butter melts, add chicken and garlic ginger paste. Stir-fry the chicken. Remove from the wok and keep aside.

3. To the same wok, add the remaining butter. Add carrots, bell pepper, cabbage, snap peas, green peas, and bell pepper. Sauté for a couple of minutes.

4. Add rice, soy sauce, scrambled eggs, chicken, celery, green onions, salt and pepper. Add ajinomoto if you are using.

5. Heat thoroughly. Serve immediately or pack in your airtight lunch box.

You can make this with leftover rice too.

Chickpeas and Sweet corn Burgers

Prep Time: 15 minutes

Ingredients:

For the patty:

- 1/4 cup canned chickpeas, drained
- 2 tablespoons canned sweet corn, drained
- 1 spring onion, chopped
- 1/8 teaspoon ground cumin
- 1 tablespoon fresh whole meal bread crumbs
- 1/8 teaspoon chili powder
- 1/2 tablespoon olive oil
- 1/2 tablespoon plain flour + extra for dusting
- 1 burger bun, cut horizontally in the middle lightly toasted
- Few rocket lettuce leaves
- Salt to taste

For the sauce:

- 1/3 cup canned tomatoes, chopped
- 1 clove garlic, crushed
- 1/8 teaspoon smoked paprika
- A pinch sugar

Instructions:

1. Add chickpeas, sweet corn, breadcrumbs, spring onions, cumin, chili, flour, and salt to a food processor. Pulse until the mixture is well combined.

2. Dust your hands and shape the mixture into a patty. Chill in the refrigerator for 15-20 minutes.

3. Meanwhile make the sauce as follows: Add tomatoes, garlic, paprika and sugar to a small pan. Place the pan

over low heat. Simmer until the sauce is thick. Adjust the seasonings if necessary.

4. Place a nonstick frying pan over medium heat. Add oil. Place the patty in the pan when the oil is heated. Cook until the bottom side is golden brown. Flip sides and cook the other side too.

5. To serve: Apply the sauce on the slit part of the bun. Place a few rocket leaves. Place the patty over the leaves. Cover with the other half of the bun.

6. Serve immediately or pack in your lunch box.

Tomato Sandwich

Prep Time: 5 minutes

Ingredients:

- 4 slices bread (remove the crust if desired)
- 2-3 tablespoons mayonnaise
- Salt to taste
- Pepper to taste
- 8 thick tomato slices

Instructions:

1. Spread mayonnaise over the bread slices.

2. Place the tomatoes over 2 slices of bread. Season with salt and pepper.

3. Cover with the remaining 2 slices of bread. Cut into a desired shape.

4. Serve immediately or pack in your lunch box.

Hot dog bun Pizza

Prep Time: 10 minutes

Ingredients:

- 2-3 tablespoons pizza sauce
- 1 tablespoon green bell pepper, chopped
- 2 tablespoons fresh tomato, chopped
- 1 hot dog bun, slit horizontally in the middle
- 2 tablespoons onions, chopped
- 1 teaspoon oregano
- 1/4 cup mozzarella cheese, grated

Instructions:

1. Apply pizza sauce on the cut part of the bun.
2. Sprinkle bell pepper, tomatoes and onions.
3. Sprinkle oregano and cheese.
4. Bake in a preheated oven at 350 degree F for about 5 minutes until cheese melts.
5. Serve immediately or pack in your lunch box.

Cuban Sandwich

Prep Time: 3 to 5 minutes

Ingredients:

- 2 slices of whole wheat bread
- 4 to 6 slices of baked ham
- 2 slices of cheese of your choice
- 2 slices of dill pickle
- 1/2 tsp butter
- mustard

Instructions:

1. On a plate, lay the two slices of bread and spread a thin layer of mustard on one side of each.

2. Place one slice of each ingredient on top of each slice of bread, beginning with the ham, followed by the cheese and finally the pickle slices.

3. Sandwich the two sets of layers together.

4. Butter the outer part of the sandwich.

5. Heat a nonstick frying pan over medium. Place the sandwich in and press it down using a spatula for 1 to 2 minutes. Flip and repeat.

6. Remove from the pan once the sandwich is golden brown and the cheese has melted. Eat immediately or wrap in tin foil as packed lunch.

Good-for-one Tuna Spaghetti

Prep Time: 20 minutes

Ingredients:

- 1 fistful of spaghetti pasta
- 1/2 cup marinara sauce
- 2 Tbsp. parmesan cheese
- 1 small can of tuna (in brine or oil)
- 1 small red onion, sliced thinly
- 2 cloves garlic, crushed and diced
- Salt and paper
- Optional: brown sugar
- Olive oil

Instructions:

1. Heat a small pot full of water on the stove or hot plate. Add a dash of salt and a drizzle of oil. Let it boil.

2. Once it starts to boil, place your pasta into the water; it's alright if half of the strands are not submerged because they will eventually once the lower half starts to soften. Follow the manufacturer's instructions on how long the pasta should be boiled.

3. Remove pasta when al dente and drain. Set aside.

4. Drain the tuna.

5. Heat a nonstick pan on low-medium. Add a drizzle of olive oil. Sautee onion and garlic.

6. After the onions have become translucent, add the tuna and a dash of salt and pepper. Cook until tuna becomes a bit dry.

7. Add the marinara sauce and stir. Taste your sauce to check the flavor. You can add some brown sugar if you want to make it a bit sweet.

8. Remove the sauce once it is thoroughly heated and pour over your pasta. Add parmesan cheese on top. Eat immediately or pack in an airtight container for lunch on-the-go.

Broiled Tomato Sandwich

Prep Time: 1o minutes

Ingredients:

- 1 large or 2 small ripe tomatoes, sliced
- 1/2 Tbsp olive oil
- 1/2 Tbsp balsamic vinegar
- 1/2 Tbsp mayonnaise
- A pinch of dried parsley and dried oregano

- A pinch of black pepper
- 1/2 Tbsp Parmesan Cheese
- 2 slices of whole wheat bread

Instructions:

1. Lightly toast the two slices of bread.
2. Preheat toaster oven to broil.
3. Whisk olive oil and vinegar together in a small bow. Soak sliced tomatoes in marinade.
4. In another bowl, create a spread with the mayonnaise, black pepper, oregano, parsley and some of the Parmesan cheese. Spread over toast.
5. Put the marinated tomatoes on top of the toast with spread and sprinkle the rest of the Parmesan cheese on top.
6. Put the toast with the tomatoes on your toaster tray and broil for 3 to 5 minutes or until the cheese turns golden brown. You can sandwich the two slices together and wrap it in tin foil if you plan to pack it for lunch.

Bacon Mushroom Chicken

Prep Time: 1 hour and 5 minutes.

Ingredients:

- 1 boneless chicken breast
- 1 or 2 thick strips of bacon
- 1 Tbsp melted butter
- 1/2 tsp salt
- Dash of garlic powder
- 1/4 cup mushrooms, sliced into halves
- 3 Tbsp heavy cream

Instructions:

1. Preheat oven to 350 degrees F (or 175 degrees C).

2. Spread the melted butter into a small, deep baking dish that is big enough to fit your chicken breast. Place the chicken breast in the dish with the skin side facing downward.

3. Season chicken with salt and garlic powder. Turn and season the other side. Lay bacon strips over the chicken and top with mushrooms.

4. Bake in the oven for 45 to 60 minutes, or until the chicken juices come out clear.

5. Take the bacon mushroom chicken out onto a plate.

6. Collect the juices and pour into a small pan. Add heavy cream and whisk over low heat until you get a thick sauce. Pour over the chicken. Enjoy!

Classic BLT

Prep Time: 10 minutes

Ingredients:

- 2 slices of whole wheat bread
- 2 lettuce leaves
- 2 tomato slices
- 4 bacon strips
- 1 Tbsp mayonnaise

Instructions:

1. Place a nonstick pan over medium-high heat and cook bacon strips until brown. Drain the oil and places strips on paper towels.

2. Toast the bread slices.

3. Layer the bacon strips, lettuce and tomato slices on a slice of toast and spread mayonnaise on one side of the other toast. Sandwich slices together. Pack it up in tin foil to keep warm, otherwise eat immediately.

Chapter 6 - Classic and Delectable Dinner Recipes

Dinner should be a truly enjoyable experience, even if it is only yourself and your favorite music or TV show. Make dining at home an everyday luxury without overspending by cooking any one of these delectable recipes and pairing the dish with a glass of wine and a dinner roll or two. And if you really like the recipe then you can go ahead and double up the ingredients, then pack it up for reheating at lunchtime the next day.

Seafood Pasta

Prep Time: 25 minutes

Ingredients:

- 1 tomato,
- 100 grams fusilli pasta, cooked according to instruction on package but cook for 2 minutes lesser than that mentioned
- 2 cloves garlic, sliced
- 50 grams king prawn, deveined
- 50 grams scallops, halved
- 150 grams mussels, shells cleaned
- A pinch saffron soaked in 2 tablespoons hot water
- 75 ml white wine
- Zest of half a lemon
- 1 tablespoon lemon juice

- 2 tablespoons thin cream
- 1/2 teaspoon Italian seasoning
- A pinch salt
- 2 tablespoons parsley, chopped
- 1 tablespoon pine nuts, toasted

Instructions:

1. Blanch the tomato for 15 seconds in hot water. Remove with a slotted spoon and drop it into a bowl of cold water for about 30 seconds. Peel the tomato, quarter it, deseed it, and finally chop it into small pieces.
2. Place a pan over medium heat. Add oil. When the oil is hot, add garlic and sauté until light golden brown. Keep it aside.
3. Add prawns and scallops and sauté for a couple of minutes until the prawns are pink and the scallops are light golden brown. Remove and keep aside.
4. To the same pan, add the browned garlic, mussels, wine, saffron and seasoning. Cover and cook for 2-3 minutes or until the mussels open. Discard any mussels that do not open.
5. Add lemon zest, juice, salt and cream. Adjust the seasoning and salt if necessary.
6. Add pasta, prawns, scallops and tomatoes. Toss well and heat thoroughly.
7. Add parsley and pine nuts, mix well and serve.

Halibut Steak

Prep Time: 10 minutes

Ingredients:

- 1/2 pound halibut steak
- 1 clove garlic, minced
- 1/2 tablespoon brown sugar
- 1 tablespoon butter
- Black pepper powder to taste
- Salt to taste
- 1/2 tablespoon lemon juice
- 1 teaspoon soy sauce

Instructions:

1. Add butter, sugar, garlic, lemon juice soy sauce, salt and pepper to a small saucepan.
2. Place over low heat until the sugar is dissolved. Stir once in a while.
3. Grease a grill plate. Spread the sauce over the halibut and place in a preheated grill.
4. Cook for about 5 minutes each side or until the fish when pricked with a fork flakes easily.
5. Serve immediately.

Salmon with Tomatoes

Prep time: 15 minutes

Ingredients:

- 1 salmon fillet (6 ounces)
- 1 1/2 tablespoons garlic oil
- 1/2 cup uncooked white rice, long grain
- 1 cup water
- 1/4 teaspoon dried dill

- A large pinch salt
- A large pinch pepper powder
- 1/8 teaspoon paprika or to taste
- 1 tomato, diced
- 1 teaspoon garlic, minced
- 1/2 teaspoon lemon juice
- 1 1/2 tablespoons fresh parsley, chopped
- 1 tablespoon butter
- 2 tablespoons parmesan cheese
- 1 teaspoon hot sauce or to taste

Instructions:

1. Add rice and water to a medium size saucepan. Place the saucepan over medium heat and bring to a boil.
2. Lower heat, cover and cook until the rice is tender.
3. Sprinkle dill, paprika, salt and pepper over the salmon.
4. Place a skillet over medium heat. Add oil. When the oil is hot add salmon. Cook on both the side until it begins to break. Using the spatula, break the salmon into smaller pieces.
5. Add garlic, tomatoes, and lemon juice. Cook until the salmon flakes when pierced with a fork.
6. Add butter, cheese, parsley and hot sauce and cook for a couple of minutes.
7. Place the rice in a serving plate. Top with the cooked salmon and serve.

Quick Fish Curry

Prep Time: 5 minutes

Ingredients:

- 2 white fish fillets, skinned, chopped into chunks
- 1 medium onion, chopped
- 1 clove garlic, chopped
- 1/2 tablespoon vegetable oil
- 1 tablespoon curry paste
- 1/2 cup stock
- A pinch of salt or to taste
- Cooked rice to serve

Instructions

1. Place a pan over medium heat. Add oil. When the oil is heated, add onions and garlic and sauté until the onions are translucent.
2. Add curry paste and sauté for a couple of minutes. Add tomatoes and stock and bring to a boil.
3. Reduce heat and add fish. Simmer until the fish is cooked. (It should flake easily when pricked with a fork)
4. Serve hot with rice.

Quick and Easy Spanish Paella

Prep Time: 5 minutes

Ingredients:

- 50 grams chorizo, chopped
- 200 grams frozen seafood mix, defrosted
- 1/4 cup frozen green peas
- 150 grams long grain rice

- 1/2 teaspoon turmeric
- 1 small onion, sliced
- 1/2 tablespoon olive oil
- A pinch saffron
- 1/2 liter fish or chicken stock
- A pinch smoked paprika
- 1/2 teaspoon salt
- Lemon wedges to serve

Instructions:

1. Place a deep pan over medium heat. Add oil. When the oil is hot, add onions and sauté until translucent. Add chorizo and sauté for a couple of minutes.
2. Add turmeric and rice and sauté until well coated. Add saffron and paprika.
3. Add salt and stock and bring to a boil. Reduce heat, cover and simmer until most of the water is dried. Add peas. Cover and cook for 5 minutes.
4. Add seafood mixture. Cover and cook until done.
5. Serve hot with lemon wedges.

Chicken and Mushroom Skillet

Prep Time: 15 minutes

Ingredients:

- 1 tablespoon olive oil
- 1 1/2 tablespoon butter
- 1 chicken breast half, skinless, boneless, sliced
- 1/4 pound asparagus, trimmed, cut into thirds
- 1 clove garlic, minced
- 1/4 teaspoon dried basil
- 1/4 teaspoon dried parsley
- 1/8 teaspoon dried oregano
- 1 teaspoon white cooking wine
- 1 teaspoon lemon juice
- 1/8 teaspoon salt
- 1/2 cup mushroom, sliced

Instructions:

1. Place a skillet over medium high heat. Add butter. When butter melts, add chicken, parsley, basil, oregano, garlic, salt, wine and lemon juice.
2. Sauté until the chicken is brown.
3. Lower heat to medium cook for about 10 minutes until the chicken is cooked from inside.
4. Add asparagus and sauté until asparagus changes its color to bright green and is getting tender.
5. Add mushrooms and mix well. Cook for 2-3 minutes and serve immediately.

Chicken Cordon Bleu

Prep Time: 10 minutes

Ingredients:

- 1 chicken breast, skinless, boneless, trimmed, tenders removed
- 1 teaspoon extra virgin olive oil, divided
- 1 tablespoon whole wheat bread crumbs, coarsely powdered
- 1 teaspoon fresh parsley or thyme chopped
- 1 tablespoon ham, chopped
- 1/8 teaspoon salt
- Ground pepper powder to taste
- 1/2 tablespoon low fat cream cheese
- 1 1/2 tablespoons Swiss cheese

Instructions:

1. Season chicken with salt and pepper.
2. Mix together in a bowl cheese and cream cheese.
3. In another bowl, mix together breadcrumbs, 1/2-teaspoon oil and a pinch of pepper powder.
4. Add 1/2-teaspoon oil to an ovenproof nonstick skillet. Place the skillet over medium heat. Add chicken to it. Cook until browned on both the sides.
5. Spread the cheese mixture over the chicken. Sprinkle the ham pieces over the cheese layer.
6. Finally sprinkle breadcrumbs.
7. Transfer the skillet to a preheated oven. Bake in a preheated oven at 330 degree F until the chicken is no

longer pink at the center.

Chicken and Potatoes

Prep Time: 10 minutes

Ingredients:

- 2 chicken thighs (4 ounces each), skinless, boneless
- 1/2 pound red potatoes, thinly sliced
- 1 small green bell pepper, chopped
- 1/4 cup onions, chopped
- 1 clove garlic, minced
- 1 teaspoon paprika
- 1/4 teaspoon dried thyme
- 1/2 teaspoon Worcestershire sauce
- 1/4 teaspoon salt, divided
- 1/8 teaspoon ground black pepper
- 1/4 cup low sodium chicken broth
- A few sprigs of thyme

Instructions:

1. Mix together half the salt, pepper powder, paprika, thyme and Worcestershire sauce. Apply this mixture over the chicken and rub well.
2. Mix together the remaining salt, potatoes, bell pepper, onion, oil and garlic in another bowl.
3. Place a nonstick skillet over medium high heat. Transfer the potato mixture into the skillet. Sauté for 4-5 minutes. Stir occasionally.
4. Add broth and bring to a boil.

5. Lower heat, cover and cook for 5 minutes.
6. Uncover, add the chicken thighs. Mix well. Cover again and cook until the chicken and potatoes are tender.
7. Garnish with sprigs of thyme and serve.

Twenty Minute Chili

Prep Time: 10 minutes

Ingredients:

- 1 teaspoon vegetable oil
- 1/4 cup onions, chopped
- 1/4 cup green bell pepper, chopped
- 1/8 pound ground turkey breast
- 1/2 teaspoon Worcestershire sauce
- 1/8 teaspoon ground cumin
- 1 teaspoon chili powder
- 3 1/2 ounces canned kidney beans, rinsed, drained
- 1/8 teaspoon salt or to taste
- 1/8 teaspoon pepper powder or to taste
- 1/8 teaspoon dried oregano
- 3 1/2 ounces canned Mexican style stewed tomatoes with jalapeno peppers and spices, undrained
- 1/4 cup canned tomato juice
- 1 tablespoon low fat cheddar cheese, shredded
- 1 cup cooked rice or as much as required

Instructions:

1. Place a nonstick skillet over medium heat. Add oil. When oil is heated, add onions, bell pepper and turkey. Sauté

until done. Crumble the turkey with the spatula. Add rest of the ingredients except rice and cheese. Mix well and bring to a boil.

2. Cover and lower heat. Simmer for about 10 minutes.

3. Serve the chili over cooked rice. Garnish with cheese.

Turkey Fried Rice

Prep Time: 20 minutes

Ingredients:

- 1 cup cooked long grained white rice
- 1/2 tablespoon canola oil
- 1/8 pound ground turkey
- 1 scallion, sliced + extra for garnishing
- 1 carrot, sliced
- 1 teaspoon garlic, chopped
- 1 teaspoon ginger, chopped
- 1/4 cup frozen peas, thawed
- 2 teaspoons hoisin sauce
- 1/4 cup snow peas, halved
- 1/2 tablespoon rice wine vinegar

Instructions:

1. Place a nonstick skillet over medium high heat. Add oil. When the oil is hot, add scallions and sauté for a couple of minutes.

2. Add garlic, ginger and turkey. Sauté for a few minutes until browned; simultaneously breaking the ground turkey.

3. Add snow peas, peas, and carrots, sauté for a couple of minutes.

4. Add rice, hoisin sauce and vinegar. Stir-fry the rice until thoroughly heated.

5. Garnish with scallions and serve.

Macaroni and Cheese Bake

Prep Time: 10 minutes

Ingredients:

- 2 ounces small elbow macaroni, cook according to instructions on the package
- 1/4 cup carrots, peeled, shredded
- 1/4 pound ground sirloin
- Cooking spray
- 1/4 cup onions, chopped
- 1/2 teaspoon garlic, minced
- 1/4 cup fat free milk
- 1/4 cup tomato sauce
- 1/4 teaspoon salt, divided
- 1/8 teaspoon black pepper powder
- 1/2 tablespoon all purpose flour
- 1/2 cup low fat cheddar cheese, shredded, divided
- A pinch ground nutmeg

Instructions:

1. Spray the cooked pasta with cooking spray.

2. Place a large pan over medium high heat. Spray with cooking spray.

3. Add onions and carrots. Sauté until the onions are translucent. Add garlic and sauté until fragrant.

4. Add ground beef and cook until well browned, simultaneously breaking the beef.

5. Add tomato sauce, half the salt and pepper. Simmer until the moisture almost dries up.

6. Add pasta and mix well. Transfer into a greased baking dish.

7. Pour milk to a saucepan. Add flour, nutmeg and remaining salt. Whisk well.

8. Place the pan over medium heat. Stir constantly and cook until the sauce thickens. Add half the cheese and stir well. Transfer this over the pasta and mix well.

9. Sprinkle the remaining cheese and bake in a preheated oven at 350 degree F until light brown.

10. Let it remain in the oven for about 5 minutes before serving.

Healthy Picadillo

Prep Time: 10 minutes

Ingredients:

- 1/2 pound ground round
- 1/2 cup onions, thinly sliced
- 1 clove garlic, minced
- 1 teaspoon olive oil
- 1/2 cup yellow bell pepper, sliced into 1/4 inch thick slices, halve each slice
- 1/2 cup red bell pepper, sliced into 1/4 inch thick slices, halve each slice

- 3 tablespoons golden raisins
- 1/4 cup carrots, finely chopped
- 1/2 tablespoon balsamic vinegar
- 2 tablespoons dry white wine
- 1 bay leaf
- 1/4 teaspoon salt or to taste
- 1/8 teaspoon black pepper powder to taste
- 4 green olives, sliced
- 3 1/2 ounces canned stewed tomatoes, unsalted, undrained
- 2 ounces unsalted tomato sauce

Instructions:

1. Place a nonstick skillet over medium heat. Add beef and cook until brown simultaneously breaking the beef. Remove from the pan and keep aside.
2. To the same pan add oil. Add onions and garlic and sauté until onions are translucent. Add bell peppers and carrots and sauté for a couple of minutes.
3. Add the browned beef, raisins and rest of the ingredients. Mix well and bring to a boil.
4. Lower heat and simmer for about 8-10 minutes. Stir occasionally.
5. Discard the bay leaf and serve.

Beef Stew

Prep Time: 30 minutes + marinating

Ingredients:

- 1/4 pound beef stew meat, cut into 1 inch cubes

- 1 1/2 cups beef broth, divided
- 3/4 cup dry red wine
- 1 1/2 tablespoons lemon juice
- 1 teaspoon olive oil
- 1 teaspoon soy sauce
- 1 teaspoon Worcestershire sauce
- 1 small onion, chopped
- 2 cloves garlic, minced
- 1/2 cup baby Portobello mushrooms, sliced
- 1 medium carrot, peeled, chopped into 1 inch slices
- 1 small potato, cut into 1 inch cubes
- A pinch cayenne pepper
- 1 sprig thyme
- 1 teaspoon corn starch

Instructions:

1. Add half the wine, lemon juice, soy sauce, Worcestershire sauce and beef to a zip lock plastic bag. Seal the bag and turn it around a couple of times to coat well.
2. Place the bag in the refrigerator overnight. If possible, turn around a couple of times.
3. Next morning, discard the marinade and transfer beef to a saucepan. Add oil and cook until brown. Remove with a slotted spoon and keep aside.
4. To the same pan add onions and sauté until translucent. Add garlic and sauté for a minute. Add a cup of broth, remaining wine and beef. Bring to a boil.
5. Lower heat, cover and simmer for 15 minutes. Add potatoes, carrots, mushrooms, thyme and cayenne

pepper.

6. Cover and simmer until tender. Remove thyme sprig and discard it.

7. In a small bowl, mix cornstarch and remaining broth until smooth. Gently pour it into the stew stirring constantly until thickened.

8. Serve hot.

Spicy Beef Burger

Prep Time: 10 minutes

Instructions:

- 4 ounces lean beef mince
- 1 clove garlic, crushed
- 1/2 teaspoon mustard
- 1 small egg beaten but use only half of it
- 1/2 teaspoon tomato ketchup
- 1 tablespoon onion, finely chopped
- 1 spring onion, sliced
- 4-5 basil leaves, chopped
- 1/2 red chili, finely chopped
- Cooking spray
- A large pinch salt
- 1 whole wheat burger bun

Instruction:

1. Mix together in a bowl, beef mince, garlic, ketchup, mustard, egg, onion, green onion, salt and chili. Using your hands mix well and shape into a patty.

2. Place a nonstick pan over medium heat. Spray with cooking spray.

3. Place the patty in the pan and cook on both the sides until done or grill it.

4. Slit the bun and place the patty in it. Serve with salad and a dip of your choice.

Beef Stroganoff

Ingredients:

- 1/2 pound beef tenderloin, trimmed, chopped into bite sized pieces
- 1 1/2 tablespoons butter
- 1 1/4 cups mushrooms, sliced
- 1 cup beef broth
- 2 tablespoons shallots, finely chopped
- 1 teaspoon cornstarch
- 1/3 cup sour cream
- 1 teaspoon Dijon mustard
- A large pinch salt or to taste

Instructions:

1. Place a nonstick skillet over medium heat. Add1 tablespoon butter. When butter melts, add beef and brown on all the sides. Transfer on to a rimmed baking sheet.

2. To the same pan add butter, shallots and mushrooms and sauté until soft.

3. Add sour cream and mustard. Mix well. Transfer the beef back to the pan along with the released juices. Heat thoroughly adding salt.

4. Serve hot.

Chapter 7: Delectable Dinners – Lamb Recipes

Lamb Casserole

Prep Time: 20 minutes

Ingredients:

- 1/2 pound ground lamb
- 1/2 teaspoon ground cumin
- 1/2 teaspoon salt or to taste
- 1/2 slice crust less bread
- 2 tablespoons milk
- 1 small onion, finely chopped
- 1 small potato, thinly sliced
- 1 small tomato, thinly sliced
- 2 cloves garlic, minced
- 1/2 teaspoon sumac
- 1/4 teaspoon allspice
- 1/4 teaspoon black pepper powder
- 1/2 cup parsley, minced
- A pinch mace

Instructions:

1. Tear the bread into pieces and place it in a large bowl. Add milk to it. Mash it. Add allspice, salt, pepper, sumac, cumin, onions and garlic. Mix well.

2. Add parsley and lamb. Mix well and transfer into a small, greased baking casserole dish. Spread it all over the dish.
3. Place the casserole dish in the oven and broil until brown on top.
4. Remove from the oven.
5. Lay the potato slices all over the dish. Lay the tomato slices all over the potatoes.
6. Cover with aluminum foil.
7. Place it back in the oven and bake at 375 degree F for 40 minutes.

Pastitsio: Greek Lasagna

Prep Time: 30 minutes

Ingredients:

- 1 cup penne pasta

- 1/2 cup mozzarella cheese, shredded
- 1/4 pound ground lamb
- 1 clove garlic, minced
- 1 small onion, finely chopped
- 1/2 tablespoon olive oil
- A pinch ground nutmeg
- A pinch ground cinnamon
- 1 ounce feta cheese, crumbled
- 1/4 teaspoon dried rosemary

- 1/4 teaspoon dried oregano
- 3 1/2 ounces canned, finely diced tomatoes
- 1 tablespoon red wine
- 1/8 teaspoon salt
- A pinch pepper powder

For the sauce:
- 1 tablespoon flour
- 1 tablespoon butter
- 1/2 cup milk + more if required
- Yolk of a small egg, beaten
- 1 ounce parmegiano cheese, grated
- 1/8 teaspoon salt
- A pinch pepper powder

Instructions:

1. Cook the pasta according to the instructions on the package. Drain and rinse in cold water. Drain again.
2. Add mozzarella cheese and toss well. Keep aside.
3. Place a nonstick skillet over medium high heat. Add ground lamb. Cook until browned well.
4. Add salt and pepper. Remove and keep aside. Drain off the excess fat in the pan.
5. Lower heat to medium and add onions to the same pan. Sauté until the onions are translucent.

6. Add garlic and sauté for a few seconds until fragrant. Add wine, rosemary, oregano, cinnamon and nutmeg. Mix well and try to scrape out the stuck brown bits.

7. Add tomatoes along with the liquid and the browned lamb. Add more salt and pepper if desired. Simmer for about 10 minutes. Add feta cheese and simmer for another 3-4 minutes.

8. Add butter to a small saucepan. When butter melts, add flour and stir for a few seconds constantly until fragrant. Gently pour the milk, whisking constantly until the sauce is thick.

9. Add yolk and whisk again. Add parmegiano cheese and cook until melted. Add salt and pepper.

10. Add half the pasta to a small baking dish. Spread it all over the bottom of the dish.

11. Spread the lamb mixture over the pasta. Spread the remaining pasta over the lamb mixture.

12. Pour the sauce all over the pasta. Spread evenly.

13. Place the baking dish in a preheated oven at 350 degree F for about 20 minutes or until browned.

14. Remove from the oven. Cool for around 5 minutes and serve.

Irish Stew

Prep Time: 20 minutes

Ingredients:

- 1/2 pound lamb stew meat, cut into bite sized pieces, pat dried
- 1 small onion, chopped

- 1 small parsnip, cut into 1 inch long pieces
- 1 small turnip, cut into eighths
- 1 medium carrot, cut into 1 inch long pieces
- 1/2 cup red wine
- 1 tablespoon olive oil
- 1 cup chicken stock
- 2 tablespoons pearl barley
- 1 teaspoon red wine vinegar
- 1 tablespoon tomato paste
- 1 teaspoon juniper berries, smashed flat, finely chopped
- Salt to taste
- Pepper powder to taste

Instructions:

1. Sprinkle salt and pepper over the lamb.
2. Place a large saucepan over medium high heat. Add oil. When oil is hot, add lamb and cook the lamb until brown on all sides. Remove and keep aside.
3. To the same pan add onions and sauté until brown.
4. Add wine and raise the heat to high. Boil until wine reduces to half its quantity. Scrape the browned bits.
5. Add the meat to the pot along with all the released juices.
6. Add rest of the ingredients and bring to a boil.
7. Lower the heat to low, close with a lid leaving a gap of about 1/2 an inch. Simmer for about an hour or until the meat is cooked.
8. Adjust the seasonings if necessary. Serve hot.

Quick and easy Lamb Chops

Prep Time: 10 minutes

Ingredients:

- 2 lamb loin chops (3 ounces each)
- 1/4 teaspoon dried basil
- 1/4 teaspoon thyme
- 1/4 teaspoon dried basil
- Salt to taste

Instructions:

1. Mix together in a small bowl the dried herbs and salt. Rub this mixture all over the lamb chops.
2. Cover and refrigerate for at least an hour.
3. Place in an oven at least 4-6 inches away from the heating element. Broil 5-8 minutes per side or until done.
4. Ready to serve.

Quick Skillet Lamb

Prep Time: 10 minutes

Ingredients:

- 1 lamb leg chop
- 1 teaspoon olive oil
- 1/2 cup small button mushrooms
- 1 spring onion, chopped
- 1/2 cup canned tomatoes, chopped
- 1 tablespoon dry red wine
- 1/2 tablespoon fresh flat leaf parsley, chopped
- Soft polenta to serve

- 1 tablespoon pitted black olives

Instructions:

1. Place a nonstick skillet over medium high heat. Add oil. Add lamb chop. Cook until brown on both the sides. Remove from the skillet and keep aside.
2. To the same pan add onions and mushrooms. Sauté until browned. Add the browned lamb back to the pan along with tomatoes, tomato paste and wine. Bring to a boil.
3. Lower the heat, cover and simmer for about 5 minutes. Uncover and cook for a couple of minutes.
4. Add parsley and olives.
5. Serve hot with soft polenta.

Ham and Sweet Potatoes

Prep Time: 5 minutes

Ingredients:

- 1 ham steak
- 2 tablespoons brown sugar
- 4 ounces canned, crushed pineapple, drained
- 1/2 a 15 ounce can sweet potatoes, drained
- 1/2 cup miniature marshmallows

Instructions:

1. Take a large sheet of aluminum foil. Place the ham slice over it. Sprinkle a little brown sugar on both the sides.
2. Place the crushed pineapple over it. Place the sweet potatoes over it. Sprinkle some more brown sugar over it. Close the foil tightly all around the ham.

3. Place the wrapped ham on a baking sheet and bake in a preheated oven at 350 degree F for about 30 minutes.

4. Remove from the oven. Open the foil, which is covering the top part. Sprinkle marshmallows over the sweet potatoes and bake for 10 more minutes. Serve hot.

Pan Fried Pork Chops

Prep Time: 5 minutes

Ingredients:

- 1/2 ounce dry onion soup mix (1/2 an envelope)
- 1 pork chop
- 2 tablespoons all purpose flour
- 1/2 cup olive oil

Instructions:

1. Add onion soup powder to a bowl. Crush the larger pieces of onions into finer pieces.

2. Add flour to it. Roll the pork chop in this mixture.

3. Place a small heavy skillet over medium heat. Add oil. When the oil is hot but not smoking (put a pinch of the flour into it and if the oil sizzles immediately, then oil is ready).

4. Tap off the excess flour mixture from the chop and place the chop in the skillet. Cook on both the sides are brown and cooked. Turn the chop around a couple of times.

5. When done, remove with a slotted spoon and serve.

Chipotle Pork Tacos

Prep Time: 20 minutes

Ingredients:

- 1/4 pound pork tenderloin, trimmed
- 2 corn tortillas (6 inches each)
- 1 tablespoon low fat sour cream
- 1/2 teaspoon lemon rind, finely grated
- 1 teaspoon lime juice
- 1/4 teaspoon brown sugar
- 1/2 teaspoon fresh oregano, minced
- 1 teaspoon chipotle chili in adobo sauce
- 11/2 teaspoon minced garlic
- A large pinch salt
- 1/2 teaspoon olive oil
- Cooking spray
- 1/4 cup shallots, thinly sliced

Instructions:

1. Place the pork tenderloin in a thick zip lock plastic bag. Pound with a meat mallet until you get 1/4-inch thickness. In case you do not have a meat mallet, you can beat it with something heavy like a mortar and pestle or a rolling pin).
2. Cut the pork into thin strips.
3. Mix together pork, lime rind, garlic, shallots, lime juice, brown sugar oregano, chipotle chili and salt.
4. Place a nonstick skillet over medium high heat. Spray with cooking spray.
5. Add shallots and sauté until translucent. Transfer into a bowl and keep aside.

6. To the same pan add oil; add pork mixture and sauté for a few minutes until it is not pink any more.
7. Add pork mixture to the bowl of shallots.
8. Warm the tortillas in accordance to the instructions given on the package.
9. Divide the pork mixture amongst the tortillas. Add 1/2-tablespoon sour cream over the pork mixture on each of the tortillas.
10. Sprinkle cilantro and fold in the middle. Serve immediately.

Crispy Pork Medallions

Prep Time: 10 minutes

Ingredients:

- 1/4 pound cut into 2 medallions
- 2 tablespoons panko bread crumbs
- 1/2 tablespoon Dijon mustard
- 1 teaspoon fresh parsley, minced
- 1 teaspoon fresh thyme, minced
- 1/2 tablespoon extra virgin olive oil
- A large pinch salt or to taste
- A pinch pepper powder or to taste

Instructions:

1. Apply mustard over the pork medallions. Rub well.
2. Mix together in a bowl, panko, thyme, parsley, salt and pepper.

3. Place the medallion in the panko mixture. Coat well on both the sides.

4. Place an ovenproof skillet over medium high heat. Add oil.

5. When oil is hot, add medallions and cook until golden brown.

6. Flip sides. Place the skillet in a preheated oven and bake at 450 degree F for around 8 minutes. Let it remain in the oven for about 5 minutes before serving.

Stir-Fry Pork with Ginger

Prep Time: 15 minutes

Ingredients:

- 1/4 pound lean pork, thinly sliced
- 1 tablespoon vegetable oil
- 1/2 teaspoon sesame oil
- 1 teaspoon soy sauce
- 1/4 teaspoon salt or to taste
- A pinch sugar
- 1/2 tablespoon rice wine
- 1 leek, chopped
- 3/4 inch piece ginger, peeled, thinly sliced

Instructions:

1. Place a wok over medium heat. Add vegetable oil. When oil is hot, add ginger and sauté for around 30 seconds.

2. Add pork and sauté for a minute. Add soy sauce, sugar and salt. Mix well and cook for around 10 minutes.

3. Add sesame oil, leeks and rice wine. Lower heat and cook until pork is tender.

Ham Pizza

Prep Time: 20 minutes

Ingredients:

- 1/4 cup smoked ham, diced
- 1/2 pound pizza dough
- 1/2 tablespoon flour for dusting
- 1/2 cup fresh asparagus, trimmed
- 2 tablespoons olive oil
- 1 clove garlic, minced
- Salt to taste
- Pepper powder to taste
- A pinch red chili flakes or to taste
- 1/4 cup white cheddar cheese, shredded

- 1/2 tablespoon Parmigiano-Reggiano cheese
- 1 teaspoon fresh oregano, minced
- 1/2 teaspoon fresh basil, minced
- 1/4 cup ricotta cheese
- 1 tablespoon heavy cream

Instructions:

1. Place a large saucepan with water over medium heat and bring to a boil. Add a little salt and asparagus and cook until tender. Drain and immerse in chilled water for around 10 minutes. Drain and keep aside.
2. Mix together in a small bowl, ricotta, oil, garlic, red chili flakes, cream, salt and pepper.

3. Place the pizza dough on your work area, which is dusted with flour. Sprinkle some flour over the dough too.

4. Use a rolling pin and roll into a thin crust of about 6 inches diameter.

5. Transfer the rolled pizza crust on to a baking sheet.

6. Apply the ricotta cheese mixture all over the crust. Sprinkle herbs, ham and asparagus all over the crust. Sprinkle the cheese.

7. Bake the crust in a preheated oven at 550 degree F initially placing it on the bottom rack for 5 minutes and then placing it on the top rack for 5 minutes.

Chili Garlic Vegetable Fried Rice

Prep Time: 10 minutes

Ingredients:

- 1/2 cup rice (white or brown)
- 2 cloves garlic, minced
- 1 medium onion, chopped
- 1/2 cup mushrooms, sliced
- 1 small carrot, peeled, chopped
- 2 tablespoons green bell pepper, chopped
- 2 tablespoons red bell pepper, chopped
- 1 cup cabbage, chopped
- 1 green onion, sliced
- 1 tablespoon rice wine vinegar
- 1/2 teaspoon sesame oil
- 2 teaspoons soy sauce
- 1 teaspoon hot sauce

- Salt to taste
- Pepper powder to taste
- 4-5 green beans, thinly sliced
- 1/2 tablespoon vegetable oil

Instructions:

1. Cook rice according to instructions on the package.
2. Place a wok or large skillet over medium high heat. Add vegetable oil. When the oil is hot, add onions and garlic and sauté until the onions are translucent.
3. Add carrots and beans, sauté for a couple of minutes.
4. Add mushrooms, bell peppers, and cabbage. Sauté for a couple of minutes.
5. Add green onions, salt, pepper, soy sauce and hot sauce. Mix well. Add cooked rice and heat thoroughly. Add vinegar, mix well and remove from heat.
6. Add sesame oil, mix well and serve.

Spring Vegetable Ragout

Prep Time: 10 minutes

Ingredients:

- 2 ounces whole grain spaghetti
- 1/2 yellow summer squash, cut into bite sized pieces
- 1/2 cup sugar snap peas, cut in half
- 1/2 tablespoon extra virgin olive oil
- 1/4 cup vegetable broth
- 8 cherry tomatoes, halved
- 6 tablespoons parmesan cheese, finely grated

- 1 small leek, white and pale green parts only
- 1 tablespoon fresh basil leaves, minced
- 1/4 teaspoon salt or to taste
- 1/8 teaspoon black pepper powder

Instructions:

1. Cook the spaghetti according to the instructions on the package. Keep aside.
2. Meanwhile place a saucepan over medium heat. Add oil. When the oil is hot, add leek and sauté for a couple of minutes.
3. Add squash and snap peas and sauté until slightly tender.
4. Add tomatoes and broth and bring to a boil. Cook for about a minute and add pepper, salt and basil. Stir-fry for a minute more.
5. Remove from heat. Add cheese and mix well.
6. Add pasta, toss well and serve.

Vegetable omelet

Prep Time: 15 minutes

Instructions:

- 1 green onion, chopped
- 1 small red potato, diced, boiled in a small saucepan of salted water
- 2 tablespoons mushrooms, sliced
- 1 tablespoon yellow bell pepper, chopped
- 1 tablespoon red bell pepper, chopped
- 2 tablespoons tomatoes, chopped
- 1/2 tablespoon olive oil

- Salt to taste
- Pepper powder to taste
- 1/3 cup egg substitute
- 1 tablespoon fat free sour cream
- 2 tablespoons low fat cheddar cheese, divided
- Cooking spray

Instructions:

1. Place a skillet over medium heat. Add oil. When oil is hot, add mushrooms, bell peppers, green onion and potatoes. Sauté until the vegetables are tender. Remove from heat. Add half the cheese and stir.
2. Place a nonstick skillet over medium heat. Spray with cooking spray. Pour the egg substitute. Cook until set.
3. Spread the cooked vegetables mixture all over it. Sprinkle cheese and serve.

Walnut and Cheese Tortellini

Prep Time: 10 minutes

Ingredients:

- 4 1/2 ounces refrigerated cheese tortellini
- 3 tablespoons walnuts, chopped, toasted
- 1/4 cup butter, cubed
- 1/4 cup fresh parsley, minced
- 1/3 cup parmesan cheese, shredded
- 1/8 teaspoon coarsely ground pepper
- A pinch salt or to taste

Instructions:

1. Cook the tortellini according the instructions on the package, drain and keep warm.
2. Place a pan over medium heat. Add butter. When butter melts, add tortellini, parsley and walnuts. Toss well.
3. Sprinkle cheese, salt and pepper.

Delicata Squash and Tofu Curry

Prep Time: 15 minutes

Ingredients:

- 1/2 a small delicata squash, seeded, chopped into 1 inch cubes
- 4 ounces extra firm tofu, pat dried, chopped into 1 inch cubes
- 2 cups chard or kale, chopped, remove the hard stems
- 2 teaspoons canola oil, divided
- 1/2 tablespoon curry powder
- 1 small onion, halved, sliced
- 1/2 teaspoon fresh ginger, grated
- 7 tablespoons light coconut milk
- 1/4 teaspoon light brown sugar
- 1/2 tablespoon lime juice
- 1/4 teaspoon salt or to taste
- 1/8 teaspoon pepper or to taste
- Hot cooked rice to serve

Instructions:

1. Mix together curry powder, salt and pepper. Add half teaspoon of this mixture to the tofu and keep aside. Toss

well and keep aside.

2. Place a nonstick skillet over medium high heat. Add 1-teaspoon oil. When the oil is hot, add tofu and cook until browned. Remove from the pan and keep aside.

3. To the same pan, add the remaining oil. Add onions and sauté until the onions are translucent.

4. Add ginger, squash and the remaining curry powder mixture. Cook until the vegetables are light brown. Add coconut milk and brown sugar and bring to a boil.

5. Add half the kale and cook until it wilts slightly.

6. Add tofu and the remaining kale. Cook until the squash is tender.

7. Remove from heat and add lime juice.

8. Serve with hot rice.

Baked Salmon

Prep Time: 3 minutes preparation, 1 hour marination, and 45 minutes baking time

Ingredients:

- 1 clove garlic, minced
- 3 Tbsp olive oil
- 1/2 tsp dried basil
- 1/2 tsp salt
- 1/2 tsp ground black pepper
- 1/2 Tbsp lemon juice
- 1/2 Tbsp chopped fresh parsley
- 1 6-oz. Fillet salmon

Instructions:

1. Combine the lemon juice, salt and pepper, olive oil, garlic and parsley in a small bowl.
2. Place the fillet in a glass baking dish and pour the marinade on top.
3. Marinate in the refrigerator or cooler for 30 minutes, turn the fillet over, and then marinate for another 30 minutes.
4. Preheat oven to 375 degrees F (or 190 degrees C).
5. Put the salmon fillets in tin foil along with the marinade, then close the tin foil tightly. Put in a glass dish and into the oven.
6. Bake for 45 minutes or until fillet can easily be flaked.

Baked Falafel

Prep Time: 30 minutes

Ingredients:

- 1 egg
- 1 small onion, chopped
- Half a can of garbanzo beans (place the other half in an airtight container with the juices and refrigerate)
- 3 Tbsp chopped fresh parsley
- 1 clove garlic
- 1/2 tsp ground cumin
- A pinch of ground coriander, salt and baking soda
- 1/2 Tbsp all-purpose flour
- 1 tsp olive oil

Instructions:

1. Rinse and drain the garbanzo beans.
2. Beat the egg until foamy.

3. Place onion between two sheets of heavy duty kitchen towels and press hard to get rid of moisture. Set aside.

4. Using a food processor, coarsely puree garbanzo beans, parsley, garlic, coriander, salt and baking soda. Combine the mixture with the onion.

5. Add the beaten egg and flour into the mixture and form into two large balls. Flatten the balls on a plate and set aside for 15 minutes.

6. Preheat oven to 400 degrees F (or 200 degrees C).

7. Place an oven-safe frying pan over medium-high heat. Drizzle olive oil in pan and fry patties until golden brown on both sides.

8. Place the skillet into the oven and bake for 10 minutes. Enjoy!

Savory Garlic Steaks

(If possible, marinate steaks in fridge/cooler for 25 to 48 hours before cooking.)

Prep Time: 20 to 30 minutes.

Ingredients:

- 1 1/2-lb. rib-eye steak
- 1/4 cup balsamic vinegar
- 3 Tbsp soy sauce
- 1 1/2 Tbsp minced garlic
- 1 Tbsp honey
- 1 Tbsp olive oil
- 1 tsp black pepper
- 1/2 tsp Worcestershire sauce
- 1/2 tsp onion powder

- A pinch of salt
- A pinch of cayenne pepper
- Optional: 1/4 tsp liquid smoke flavoring

Instructions:

1. Combine the vinegar, soy sauce, Worcestershire sauce, honey, olive oil, garlic, black pepper, onion powder, salt, cayenne pepper and liquid smoke in a small bowl.
2. In a shallow dish, put the steak in and pour the marinade on top. Coat the entire steak and rub it into the meat. Cover the dish and allow to marinate in the fridge or cooler for 24 to 48 hours.
3. Place grill on medium-high heat.
4. Spray or brush some oil on the grill and grill the steak for 7 minutes for each side. Rub some of the marinade on the steak as you grill. Enjoy!

Recipe Stuffed Pork Chops with Apple and Gorgonzola

Prep Time: 1 hr and 30 minutes

Ingredients:

- 1 thick cut pork chop
- 1/4 cup chopped Granny Smith apples
- 2 Tbsp Gorgonzola cheese, crumbled
- 1/2 Tbsp butter
- 1 tsp dried thyme
- 1 clove garlic, minced
- A drizzle of olive oil
- 1 1/2 Tbsp dry sherry

- 1 Tbsp heavy cream
- 3 Tbsp chicken broth
- Salt and black pepper

Instructions:

1. Preheat the oven to 375 degrees F (or 190 degrees C).
2. Prepare the apple stuffing: put a frying pan on medium heat, put the butter in and saute the chopped apples, thyme and add a pinch of salt and pepper for 15 minutes or until apple softens.
3. Put mixture in a bowl and add 1 tablespoon of Gorgonzola cheese. Mix well.
4. Cut the pork chop across from the fat to the bone to make a butterfly cut. Stuff the center with the apple mixture. Set aside 1 or 2 tablespoons of the mixture.
5. Bake the pork chop for 60 minutes.
6. Remove pork chop from the oven and place on a plate. Add the remaining apple mixture around the chop.
7. Place a nonstick pan over low heat and saute the garlic. Add the cheese and allow to melt. Add sherry, cream, half of the chicken stock, and a pinch of salt and pepper. Mix well.
8. Stir until sauce starts to thicken. Add the rest of the chicken stock and stir. Drizzle the sauce over the pork chop.

Pita Chicken

Prep Time: 15 minutes

Ingredients:

- 1 skinless and boneless chicken breast

- 1/2 Tbsp olive oil
- A dash of garlic powder and onion powder
- A dash of salt, black pepper and cayenne pepper
- 2 Tbsp salsa
- 1 pita bread
- 1 tomato, diced
- 1/2 cup shredded lettuce
- 1/4 cup avocado, sliced
- 1 Tbsp low fat sour cream

Instructions:

1. Slice the chicken breast into strips.
2. Heat a small nonstick frying pan over low-medium and pour in oil. Saute chicken, then add salt, pepper, cayenne pepper, onion powder and garlic powder.
3. Add salsa and let simmer until chicken is completely cooked.
4. Cut pita in half and spoon chicken into pocket. Add tomatoes, lettuce, avocado and sour cream. Enjoy!

Pasta with Swiss Chard

Prep Time: 20 to 25 minutes

Ingredients:

- a handful of Angel's hair pasta (preferably whole wheat)
- 1 Tbsp olive oil
- 1 clove garlic
- 1/2 tsp capers
- 1 small bunch of Swiss chard

- 1 tsp lemon juice
- 1 Tbsp grated Parmesan cheese

Instructions:

1. Chop the Swiss chard and mince the garlic.
2. Fill a small pot with water and add some oil and salt. Let boil over high heat.
3. Add pasta and cook uncovered. Follow manufacturer's instructions as to how long it should be in the pot to get al dente.
4. Drain the pasta and set aside.
5. Heat olive oil in a small nonstick pan over medium. Saute the garlic until translucent, then add Swiss chard and stir until tender. Add a bit of pasta water to help steam and soften the chard.
6. Add the pasta to the olive oil and chard mixture. Add the capers and season with salt and pepper.
7. Transfer to a plate and add lemon juice. Sprinkle Parmesan cheese on top and enjoy!

Chapter 8: Scrumptious and Healthy Snack and Dessert Recipes

Healthy Potato Wedges

Prep Time: 5 minutes + baking time

Ingredients:

- 2 medium potatoes, rinsed, chopped into wedges
- 1 tablespoon oil
- 1/2 teaspoons mixed herbs
- A pinch of salt
- A pinch of black pepper
- A pinch of chili powder
- 1 tablespoon lemon juice

Instructions:

1. Mix together all the ingredients to coat well.
2. Bake in a preheated oven at 350 degree F for about 30 minutes or until done.
3. Serve with ketchup.

Turkey Wrap

Prep Time: 15 minutes

Ingredients:

- 1 flour tortilla (10 inches)
- 2 tablespoons cream cheese

- 1/4 cup lettuce leaves, torn
- 2 tablespoons carrots, shredded
- 1 or 2 slices deli slice turkey
- 2 tablespoons tomatoes, finely chopped
- Salt to taste
- Pepper powder to taste

Instructions:

1. Place the tortilla on a plate. Spread cream cheese all over it. Sprinkle lettuce leaves.
2. Place the turkey slices over the lettuce. Sprinkle tomatoes and carrots. Sprinkle salt and pepper.
3. Roll tightly and serve. If you like, you can chop it into smaller pieces and fasten with toothpicks.

Deviled Eggs

Prep Time: 15 minutes

Ingredients:

- 2 eggs, hard boiled, peeled, halved lengthwise
- 1/2 tablespoon mayonnaise
- 1/2 tablespoon prepared mustard
- 1/4 teaspoon garlic salt
- 1/4 teaspoon onion powder
- A pinch paprika

Instructions:

1. Remove the yolks from the eggs and place in a bowl. Keep aside the whites.

2. To the yolks, add onion powder, salt, mustard and mayonnaise and mash well.
3. Spoon this mixture into the cavity of the yolk. Sprinkle paprika.
4. Chill and serve.

Cheesy Kale Chips

Prep Time: 5 minutes + baking time

Ingredients:

- 1 bunch kale leaves, torn into large pieces
- Cooking spray
- 2 tablespoons parmesan, grated
- Salt to taste
- Paprika to taste

Instructions:

1. Lay the kale leaves on a baking sheet. Season with salt, pepper and paprika. Spray with cooking spray.
2. Bake in a preheated oven at 350 degree F until crisp. Turn around the leaves a couple of times.
3. Sprinkle Parmesan and serve warm.

Pita Pizza

Prep Time: 5 minutes + baking time

Ingredients:

- 1 pita bread
- 2 tablespoons pasta sauce
- 2 tablespoons cheese, grated

- 1 tablespoon sweet corn
- Cooking spray
- 2 cherry tomatoes, halved
- A pinch salt
- A pinch pepper powder

Instructions:

1. Apply pasta sauce on the pita bread. Place the tomatoes over it.
2. Sprinkle cheese. Spray a little olive oil. Sprinkle salt and pepper.
3. Bake in a preheated oven at 350 degree F for 10 minutes or until the cheese is light brown.

Stuffed Mushrooms

Prep Time 10 minutes

Ingredients:

- 8-10 button mushroom caps
- 2-3 tablespoons pesto
- 2-3 tablespoons ham, finely chopped

Instructions:

1. Microwave the mushrooms until slightly soft.
2. Mix together ham and pesto. Stuff it in the mushroom cavity.
3. Microwave for a few more seconds and serve.

Smoked Turkey rolls

Prep Time: 5 minutes

Ingredients:

- 2 slices smoked turkey breast
- 1 tomato, thinly sliced
- 2-3 tablespoons cream cheese, softened
- A pinch salt
- A pinch pepper powder

Instructions:

1. Place the turkey slices on your work area. Spread cream cheese over it.
2. Place tomatoes. Season with salt and pepper.
3. Roll tightly. Chop into 1 inch pieces and serve.

Snacking in between meals is the best way to curb those food cravings and keep that nasty food binge away. Likewise, there is no harm in indulging yourself in a delectable dessert that is just enough for one. Have fun whipping up and digging into these tasty snacks and dessert recipes. If you have a fridge, or if you have some friends over, you can double or even triple the measurements.

Butterscotch Pudding

Prep Time: 10 minutes, 3 hrs freezing time

Ingredients:

- 1/4 cup whole milk
- 1/2 Tbsp cornstarch
- 1/3 cup 2 percent reduced-fat milk
- 1 Tbsp dark brown sugar
- 1/3 tsp vanilla extract

- A pinch of salt
- 1 medium-sized egg yolk
- 1 tsp cold butter

Instructions:

1.

Mix some of the whole milk and cornstarch in a bowl using a fork or whisk.

2.

Combine the rest of the whole milk with the 2-percent milk in a small pan over medium heat. Let simmer.

3.

Add the vanilla extract, brown sugar, salt, and egg yolk to the cornstarch mixture. Mix well. Slowly add the heated milk to the mixture while constantly whisking.

4.

Transfer mixture into a small pan and cook over medium heat. Let boil while constantly whisking.

5.

Cook mixture until it thickens. Always stir.

6.

Remove from heat and stir in butter until it melts.

7.

Transfer into a glass or container and place into the fridge or cooler. Cover with plastic wrap and chill for at least 180 minutes before eating.

Peach Mango Smoothie

Prep Time: 5 minutes

Ingredients:

- 1 6-oz container of organic fat-free yogurt
- 1 tsp honey or agave syrup
- 1/4 cup frozen sliced peaches
- 1/4 cup peach nectar
- 1/4 cup frozen mango pieces

Instructions:

1.
Put all of the ingredients in a blender and blend until smooth; or mix together in a bowl for a chunky dessert.
2.
Eat immediately after preparing.

Hazelnut Cheesecake Parfaits

Prep time: 25 minutes + chilling

Ingredients:

- 2 tablespoons hazelnuts
- 1/4 teaspoon sugar
- 1 tablespoon half and half cream
- 1 tablespoon whipped cream cheese
- 3 tablespoons semi sweet chocolate chips
- 1 whole graham chocolate cracker, crushed
- 1 teaspoon brown sugar
- 1/3 cup whipped topping + extra for topping
- 1/4 cup coffee yogurt
- 1/8 teaspoon vanilla extract
- Chocolate curls for garnished

Instructions:

1. Place a small heavy pan over medium heat. Add hazelnuts and toast it for about 3 - 4 minutes. Add sugar and mix well until sugar is melted and coats the hazelnuts.

2. Transfer on a foil and set aside to cool.

3. Add chocolate chips and cream to a small saucepan. Place the saucepan over low heat. Simmer until well blended. Remove from heat and keep aside to cool.

4. In a small bowl, add cream cheese and brown sugar. Beat well. Add yogurt and vanilla. Mix well. Add whipped topping and fold well.

5. Place the crushed graham cracker in a parfait glass. Next add the yogurt mixture followed by chocolate mixture followed by hazelnuts.

6. Chill in the refrigerator.

7. Before serving, top with whipped topping and garnish with chocolate curls.

Chocolate Mousse Towers

Prep Time: 15 minutes

Ingredients:

- 1 tablespoon instant chocolate fudge pudding mix
- 1 tablespoon chocolate syrup
- 3 chocolate wafers
- 3 tablespoons chilled heavy whipping cream
- 1 tablespoon cold milk
- Whipped cream to garnish
- Chocolate shavings to garnish

Instructions:

1. Whisk together cream, milk and pudding mix until stiff peaks are formed. Transfer into an icing bag.
2. Pour chocolate syrup over the serving plate. Place a wafer over it. Squeeze some of the pudding cream mixture over the wafer.
3. Repeat with the remaining wafers to form a tower.
4. Top with whipped cream and garnish with chocolate shavings and serve.

Peaches n Cream

Prep Time: 15 minutes + baking

Ingredients:

- 1 cup peach, peeled, sliced
- 3 tablespoons sugar
- 1 tablespoon water
- 3 tablespoons heavy whipping cream
- 1/4 teaspoon vanilla extract

Instructions:

1. Place a small saucepan over medium heat. Add water and sugar and bring to a boil. Lower heat and simmer for a couple of minutes.
2. Remove from heat and add vanilla.
3. Place peach slices in a small baking dish. Add the prepared sugar syrup. Mix well to coat the peach slices.
4. Bake in a preheated oven at 350 degree F for about 30 minutes or until the peach is tender.
5. Serve warm or chilled topping with cream.

Pumpkin Streusel Custard

Prep Time: 10 minutes + Baking

Ingredients:

- 2 tablespoons brown sugar
- 1 small egg, beaten
- 1/4 teaspoon vanilla extract
- 1/8 teaspoon ground cinnamon
- A pinch ground allspice
- A pinch ground nutmeg
- A pinch ground ginger
- A pinch salt
- 1/3 cup canned pumpkin
- 1/4 cup evaporated milk

For the topping:

- 1/2 tablespoon brown sugar
- 1 teaspoon all purpose flour
- 1/8 teaspoon ground cinnamon
- 1 tablespoon pecans, chopped
- 1 teaspoon cold butter

Instructions:

1. Add brown sugar, vanilla, salt, and allspice, ginger, nutmeg and salt to the beaten egg.
2. Whisk well. Add pumpkin and evaporated milk.
3. Transfer into a small serving ovenproof bowl or ramekin.
4. Bake in a preheated oven at 325 degree F for about 20 minutes.

5. Meanwhile make the topping as follows: Mix together in a small bowl, brown sugar, flour and ground cinnamon.

6. Add butter and using your fingertips mix into a crumbly texture. Add pecans and mix again.

7. Sprinkle the prepared topping over the custard and bake for another 15 minutes or a toothpick when inserted in the center comes out clean.

Raspberry Mango Sundae

Prep Time: 10 minutes

Ingredients:

- 1/4 cup frozen raspberries, thawed
- 1/8 teaspoon lemon juice
- 1/4 cup mango, chopped
- 1/2 tablespoon sugar
- 1 scoop nonfat frozen vanilla yogurt
- 1 tablespoons nuts of your choice, toasted

Instructions:

1. Blend together raspberries and sugar. Add lemon juice and mix well.

2. Pour it over frozen vanilla yogurt. Top with mango and nuts.

3. Serve immediately.

Fruit Crumble

Prep Time: 10 minutes + Baking

Ingredients:

- 3/4 cup mixed fruit, fresh or frozen
- 1/2 tablespoon canola oil
- 1 teaspoon sugar
- 2 teaspoons brown sugar
- 1 teaspoon orange juice
- 2 tablespoon old fashioned oats
- 2 teaspoons all purpose flour, divided
- 1 1/2 tablespoons almonds, chopped
- A pinch ground cinnamon

Instructions:

1. Mix together fruit, sugar, half the flour and orange juice in an ovenproof dish.
2. Mix together oats, almonds, and brown sugar remaining flour, oil and cinnamon. Sprinkle this over the fruit.
3. Bake in a preheated oven at 400 degree F for about 20 minutes or top is golden brown.

No Bake Blackberry Cheesecake

Prep Time: 20 minutes + Chilling

Ingredients:

For the cheesecake

- 1 graham cracker, crushed
- 1/2 tablespoon unsalted butter, melted
- 1 1/2 ounces white chocolate chopped
- 3 tablespoons heavy whipping cream
- 3 ounces cream cheese, at room temperature

For blackberry sauce:

- 3 ounces fresh blackberries
- 2 teaspoons lemon juice
- 1 tablespoon powdered sugar

Instructions:

1. Mix together cracker and butter. Add to a glass and press well.
2. Add white chocolate and 1/2 tablespoon cream to a microwavable bowl. Microwave on low for 20-second pulses. Stir each time.
3. When the mixture is melted, remove from microwave and add cream cheese.
4. Beat well with an electric mixer on medium speed.
5. Add it to the glass and refrigerate.
6. Make the sauce as follows: Add all the ingredients to a small saucepan. Place the saucepan over low heat. Simmer for around 10 minutes. Remove from heat and cool.
7. Pour it over the cream cheese mixture in the glass.
8. Whip the remaining cream and top over the sauce. Garnish with blackberries and serve.

Peanut Butter and Banana Rolls

Prep Time: 5 minutes

Ingredients:

- 1 ripe banana
- 1 tsp orange juice
- 2 Tbsp peanut butter
- 1 Tbsp vanilla yogurt

- A dash of ground cinnamon
- 1/2 Tbsp honey-crunch wheat germ
- 1 flour tortilla

Instructions:

1.

Mix the peanut butter and yogurt together until smooth.

2.

Slice the banana and add orange juice. Coat slices with the juice.

3.

Spread the peanut butter and yogurt mixture on the tortilla but leave half an inch of the border uncovered.

4.

Place the banana slices on top of the coated tortilla in one layer.

5.

Add the cinnamon to the wheat germ and sprinkle over the banana and tortilla.

6.

Roll it up and slice into bite-sized pieces. Enjoy!

Recipe Hummus and Veggie Plate

Prep Time: 3 minutes

Ingredients:

- 1 Tbsp hummus (you can buy it from the grocery store; to make your own, see next recipe)
- 1 celery stalk
- 1 carrot or 5 baby carrots
- 1 small cucumber

Instructions:

1.

Cut up the carrot, celery stalk and cucumber into bite-sized sticks.

2.

Place the hummus in the center of a plate.

3.

Arrange the vegetables around the hummus. Dip one veggie stick into the hummus before eating.

Homemade Hummus

Store in the cooler or fridge in an airtight container. Can yield up to 5 servings.

Prep Time: 5 minutes

Ingredients:

- 5 Tbsp water
- 3 Tbsp olive oil
- 1/2 tsp salt
- 2 15-oz cans of chickpeas
- 1 clove garlic
- 1/4 cup freshly squeezed lemon juice
- 1/4 cup roasted sesame seed paste (tahini)
- Optional: 1/2 tsp paprika, freshly chopped flat-leaf parsley, and 1 Tbsp roasted pine nuts

Instructions:

1.

Wash and drain chickpeas.

2.

Combine water, olive oil, salt, chickpeas, lemon juice, and roasted sesame seed paste in a food processor and process until smooth.
3.

Transfer into a container and add paprika, parsley and pine nuts on top.

Pretzels with Peanut Butter and Chocolate Dip

The recipe yields up to 30 pretzels. Keep the pretzels and dip in airtight containers for future snack times.

Prep time: 45 minutes

Ingredients:

- 4 oz. Milk chocolate
- 1/4 cup peanut butter, creamy
- 30 braided pretzel twists (preferably honey-wheat)

Instructions:

1.
Place parchment paper on a tray.
2.

Put the chocolate in a heat-resistant bowl on top of a small saucepan full of water. Place on medium-high heat to melt the chocolate. Keep stirring throughout the process.
3.

Add the peanut butter and stir until combined thoroughly. Turn off the heat.
4.

Dip each pretzel into the mixture and place on the parchment paper-lined tray.
5.

Place tray in freezer for 30 minutes or cooler for 60 minutes.

6.

Store the rest of the pretzels in an airtight container in the fridge for up to 5 days.

Chapter 9: Simple Slow Cooking Recipes for One

It has been mentioned that slow cooking is a great cooking method for people who live alone. Just get yourself a nice 2-quart crock pot which can cook dishes for one to two people. Or if you already have a large slow cooker, you can also use this and freeze the leftovers for future use. Slow cooking is ideal for busy people because it allows them to do other things while the food is cooking. It is a great kitchen gadget for cooking stews, soups, and braises—dishes that are hearty and healthy. You still need to eat hearty and healthy meals even if you are eating solo.

Before you buy a slow cooker, you need to understand that it takes as much as seven to nine hours to cook dishes in a slow cooker, thus the name. This does not mean that you have to watch over the pot while it is cooking. You can use this time to finish your chores, run errands, or even go to work. You can leave the crock pot while it is cooking and when you return from work, you will already have home cooked dinner which is better for your healthy and your wallet as well.

You can buy a crock pot online or from the store. Crock pots generally don't cost too much and you can get one for just $50. Once you buy it, you can use it for a long time. Even if it needs to be repaired it wont cost you any more than $10 for its repair. Try looking for the ones that are most selling and popular and look for a size that is not too big or too small. Cleaning up will be very easy with the crock pot as you will have only one thing to wash! Most are dishwasher friendly but you will have to particularly check for it before buying.

You can use ordinary slow cooker recipes that you can easily find online or you can use recipes for small slow cookers that are good for one person or two people. This chapter will provide you with some easy to do mini crock pot recipes that you can try at home.

Slow Cooker Spaghetti and Meatballs

You probably did not know that you can cook your favourite Italian comfort food in a slow cooker—a 2-quart small cooker at that. This recipe serves two people.

Prep time: 5 minutes

Cooking time: 5 to 7 hours

Ingredients:

- A cup of spaghetti sauce
- 4 ounces of spaghetti pasta, uncooked, preferably thin
- 8 frozen meatballs, turkey or chicken

Instructions:

1.
Lightly coat the inside of the pot using a cooking spray.
2.

Pour the water and spaghetti sauce into the pot and combine. Throw in the meatballs.
3.

Cook your spaghetti with meatballs on low for 5 to 7 hours.
4.

To make sure that your spaghetti pasta will fit into your tiny pot, cut them into quarters using your hands before adding them into your meatball and spaghetti sauce mixture.
5.

Once the spaghetti pasta is added, turn the temperature setting to high and cook for another hour, making sure to stir from time to time.

6.

This is best served with side salad and garlic bread that will make it a complete meal.

Slow Cooker Potato Soup with Cheese

This is not exactly a recipe for one because it can serve up to 3 people. You can use the leftover for tomorrow by storing it in the fridge or you can easily divide this recipe by 3. This is a great comfort food that will instantly make you feel nostalgic for the days when your mom used to cook your food.

Prep time: 10 minutes

Cooking time: 6 ½ hours

Ingredients:

- 1 bag (16 ounces) diced potatoes with sliced onions, refrigerated
- 1 can (14 ounces) reduced-sodium chicken broth
- 1 stalk of small celery, chopped or diced
- 2 tablespoons of real bacon crumbles
- ½ cup of milk
- 1 tablespoon and 2 teaspoon of flour (all-purpose)
- ½ cup of water
- 1 cup of Colby jack cheese, shredded

Instructions:

1. Put these ingredients into your small crock pot: chicken broth, water, diced potatoes with sliced onions, and celery.

2. Set the slow cooker to high and cook for 2 and ½ hours or set it to low and cook for 5 hours.

3. Add the crumbled bacon into the pot and cook for another half hour on high or an hour on low to ensure that the bacon flavour is well-incorporated into the soup.

4. Using a mixing bowl, mix the milk and flour until the texture is smooth. Add this mixture into your soup and slowly stir using a wooden spoon. This will thicken the soup.

5. Cook the soup for another 20 to 30 minutes on high.

6. Once cooked, add the cheese and serve.

Oatmeal with Apple Cinnamon Crock Pot Recipe

You can start cooking this before you go to bed so that you will wake up with a healthy and yummy breakfast for one. The delicious aroma will surely wake you up! This recipe makes 2 servings.

Prep time: 10 minutes

Cooking time: 8 to 9 hours (overnight)

Ingredients:

- 1 medium-sized apple, peeled and sliced
- 1 cup of oats, preferably old-fashioned and rolled
- Half a teaspoon of cinnamon
- 2 tablespoons and 2 teaspoons of brown sugar
- 2 cups of water
- Salt to taste

Instructions:

1. Put the sliced apples into the cooker. Add the cinnamon and cinnamon into the pot and combine all the ingredients,

making sure that the cinnamon and sugar coat the apples well.

2. Add the oats into the apple mixture, then the water into the pot and add a dash of salt. Do not stir the ingredients together because all the ingredients will mix together while cooking.

3. Turn on the slow cooker to low temp and cook overnight or around 8 to 9 hours. When you wake up in the morning, just turn the cooker off. It will still be hot when you are ready to eat breakfast.

4. Before serving, be sure to stir well. You can serve this with maple syrup if you like it to be sweeter.

TIP: Use a crock pot liner before cooking for easy cleanup.

Classic Pot Roast in a Slow Cooker

This is a complete meal for one or two people. You can start cooking this in the morning and you will have a scrumptious dinner when you get back home from work.

Prep time: 15 minutes

Cooking time: 7 to 8 hours

Ingredients:

- 8 ounces of beef chuck roast
- 15 sliced baby carrots
- 3 medium or small cubed red potatoes
- ½ of medium-sized onion (make onion ring slices)
- ½ packet of onion soup mix (e.g. Lipton Recipe Secrets)

Instructions:

1. Put the baby carrots and red potatoes into the 2-quart pot. Add the beef chuck roast on top of your vegetables. On top of the beef roast, layer the onion rings evenly.

2. Pour half the content of onion soup mix into a mixing bowl and add water. Stir well to create a creamy paste-like mixture. Spread this creamy mixture onto your vegetables and beef roast mixture.

3. Cover the pot and cook for about 7 to 8 hours.

Crock Pot Chicken Dinner

If you only have chicken and some ordinary vegetable in your kitchen, this is a perfect dish to cook for dinner. It can also be considered a complete meal because it has chicken which is a great source of protein, potatoes for carbohydrates, and other vegetables for vitamins and minerals.

Prep time: 10 minutes

Cooking time: 8 hours

Ingredients:

- 2 halves of chicken breasts, boneless and skinless
- 3 medium-sized red potatoes, roughly chopped
- 10 to 15 medium-sized baby carrots, sliced into third or halves
- 1 medium-length stalk of celery, diced or chopped
- Half a cup of thawed frozen peas
- A can of chicken soup cream
- 1/8 teaspoon of garlic powder

Instructions:

1. Put all your vegetables in the bottom of your crock pot and layer the chicken breasts evenly on top.
2. Combine the cream of chicken soup and garlic powder in a separate bowl and pour into the crock pot with the vegetables and chicken breasts. Do not mix or stir.
3. Cook for about 8 hours on low setting.
4. Serve for dinner.

Crock Pot Vegetarian Mediterranean Soup

This is the perfect soup for vegetarians and for people who are trying to lose weight. Good for two people.

Prep time: 10 minutes

Cooking time: 4 hours

Ingredients:

- 1 medium-sized tomato, roughly chopped
- 1 medium-sized zucchini, roughly chopped
- 1/3 cup of onions, chopped
- 1 small pack of Boca crumbles
- 1 tablespoons of feta cheese, crumbled
- 1 clove of garlic, minced
- 1 tablespoon of freshly squeezed lemon juice
- 1/8 teaspoon of black pepper, freshly ground
- 1 can (15 ounces) vegetable broth, reduced-sodium

Instructions:

1. Mix the following ingredients in your pot: garlic, pepper, lemon juice, zucchini, tomato, onion, and broth.

2. Cover the pot and turn on the cooker at low temperature and cook for 4 to 5 hours. You can also cook it at high temperature for about a couple of hours to 2 ½ hours.

3. At the last hour of cooking, toss in the Boca crumbles into the pot. This will ensure that they will not get soggy. Once cooked, transfer the soup into two bowls and sprinkle with feta cheese before serving.

Slow Cooked Chicken Salsa with Cheese Soup

This is a delicious dish for one or two people and is best served as a filling for your enchilada or over rice.

Prep time: 5 minutes

Cooking time: 6 to 8 hours

Ingredients:

- 2 pieces chicken breast halves, boneless and skinless
- ½ cup of salsa
- 1 and ½ teaspoon of taco seasoning
- A quarter cup of sour cream, preferably light
- ½ can of condensed cheddar or nacho cheese soup

Instructions:

1. Place the chicken breast halves on the bottom of the pot and sprinkle them with your taco seasoning.

2. TIP: You can reduce the use of taco seasoning to lower sodium. In a separate bowl, combine the cheese soup and salsa then pour this into the pot over the chicken breasts. Turn the cooker to low temperature and cook for 6 to 8 hours.

3. Take the stoneware pot off the slow cooker. Be sure to use a pot holder because the stoneware is hot to touch.

4. Get the chicken and put it in a chopping board. Shred into smaller pieces using a fork. If the chicken is really tender, you do not need to take it out of the pot and use a fork to shred it because the meat will fall off by simply stirring the chicken while still in the bowl.

5. Toss the shredded chicken back into the pot and add sour cream. Serve.

Beef Stew

Prep Time: 15 minutes

Ingredients:

- ½ pound beef stew meat, chopped into chunks
- ¾ cup potatoes, peeled, cut into 1 inch cubes
- ½ cu carrots, peeled, diced
- 2 tablespoons all purpose flour
- ¼ teaspoon salt
- ¼ teaspoon black pepper powder
- ½ teaspoon onion powder
- ¼ teaspoon garlic powder
- ¾ cup beef broth
- 1 small bay leaf
- ½ teaspoon Worcestershire sauce

Instructions:

- Add flour, salt, pepper powder, onion and garlic powders, to a bowl. Add beef pieces. Coat well.
- Place the meat pieces in a 2-quart slow cooker.
- Layer with potatoes followed by the carrots.

- Mix together beef broth and Worcestershire sauce and pour it over the carrots.
- Place a bay leaf on top.
- Cover and set the slow cooker on LOW for 6 hours.
- When cooked, discard the bay leaves and mix well.
- Serve hot with bread.

Creamy Chicken and Carrots

Prep Time: 5 minutes

Ingredients:

- 1 chicken breast half (6 ounces)
- ½ pound baby carrots, halved lengthwise
- 5 ½ ounces canned cream of mushroom soup, undiluted
- 2 ounces canned mushrooms, drained
- Hot cooked rice to serve

Instructions:

1. Add all the ingredients to a slow cooker. Mix well.
2. Cover and set the slow cooker on LOW for 4-5 hours.
3. Serve over hot rice.

Beef in Onion Gravy

Prep Time: 5 minutes

Ingredients:

- 5 ½ ounces canned, condensed cream of mushroom soup
- 1 tablespoon onion soup mix
- 1/3 pound beef stew meat, cut into 1 inch pieces

- ½ tablespoon quick cooking tapioca
- 1 tablespoon beef broth

Instructions:

1. Add soup mix, mushroom soup, tapioca and broth to the pot of the slow cooker. Keep aside for 15 minutes.
2. Add beef. Mix well.
3. Cover with the lid. Set the cooker on LOW for 6 -8 hours or until beef is tender.
4. Serve over rice or noodles or mashed potatoes.

Savory Cheese Soup

Prep time: 15 minutes

Ingredients:

- 7 ½ ounces broth (chicken or vegetable)
- 1 tablespoon red bell pepper, chopped
- 1 tablespoon onions, chopped
- 2 tablespoons celery, chopped
- 2 tablespoons carrots, chopped
- 1 teaspoon butter
- A pinch black pepper powder
- 1 tablespoon all purpose flour
- 1 tablespoon cold water
- 1 ½ ounces cream cheese, cubed
- 6 tablespoons cheddar cheese, shredded
- 3 tablespoons beer or extra broth
- Croutons to serve

1. Add all the ingredients except croutons to a slow cooker.
2. Set the cooker on Low for 3-4 hours.
3. Transfer into a soup bowl. Serve with croutons.

Herbed Turkey and Wild Rice Casserole

Prep Time: 15 minutes

Ingredients:

- 3 ounces turkey breast tenderloins, cut into ¾ inch piece
- 1 slice bacon, cut into ½ inch pieces
- ¼ cup carrots, chopped
- ¼ cup celery, chopped
- 2 tablespoons onions, chopped
- 1 cup chicken broth
- ¼ cup uncooked wild rice, rinsed, drained
- 1/8 teaspoon dried marjoram leaves
- ¼ cup sour cream
- ¼ teaspoon salt or to taste
- 1/8 teaspoon pepper powder

Instructions:

1. Place a skillet over medium heat. Add bacon. Cook until bacon is crisp. Add turkey and cook until turkey is browned. Stir occasionally.
2. Add celery, onion and carrots. Sauté for a couple of minutes and transfer into the slow cooker.
3. Add rest of the ingredients except sour cream.

4. Cover and set the cooker on HIGH for 30 minutes. After 30 minutes, change the setting of cooker to LOW for 6-7 hours or until the rice is cooked.

5. Add sour cream and mix well. Serve immediately.

Chapter 10:   Easy Leftover Recipes for One

When you cook for one, you will most likely end up with leftovers. What you can do is to use these leftovers to create completely different dishes for one. You can save a lot of money because nothing is thrown away. Here are some easy leftover recipes for one that you can try at home.

Chicken and Spinach Casserole

Prep Time: 15 minutes

Ingredients:

- 1/2 cup leftover cooked chicken breast, cubed
- 1/2 cup whole wheat pasta, uncooked
- ¼ can low fat cream of chicken soup
- ½ teaspoon salt or to taste
- Pepper to taste
- ½ teaspoon seasoning of your choice
- ¼ cup low fat cottage cheese
- 3 ounces frozen chopped spinach, thawed, squeezed of its moisture
- 3 tablespoons part skim mozzarella

Instructions:

1. Cook pasta according to instructions on the package. Drain and keep aside.

2. Mix together chicken soup, chicken and seasoning in a bowl.

3. Mix together spinach, cottage cheese and 2 tablespoons mozzarella in another bowl.

4. Add the pasta into a greased baking dish. Sprinkle the chicken pieces over it. Spread spinach mixture over the chicken layer.

5. Cover with a foil and bake in a preheated oven at 350 degree F for 35 minutes.

6. Uncover. Sprinkle the remaining cheese and more if you desire and bake for another 10 minutes.

You can use leftover turkey meat or any other meat instead of chicken.

You can also use leftover pasta.

Noodles with Spinach and Tomatoes

Prep Time: 10 minutes

Ingredients:

- 1 cup leftover cooked noodles or pasta
- 1 cup spinach
- 5-6 grape tomatoes, halved
- Salt to taste
- Pepper powder to taste
- 2-3 tablespoons feta cheese, crumbled
- ½ cup leftover chicken (optional)

Instructions:

1. Place a large pan over medium heat. Add spinach and cook for a couple of minutes until spinach wilts. Add rest of the ingredients and toss well.
2. Sprinkle some more cheese and serve.

Frittata di Pasta

Prep Time: 5 minutes

Ingredients:

- 1 cup cooked spaghetti or any other leftover pasta
- Any leftover pasta sauce
- 1 egg, beaten
- 2 tablespoons parmesan cheese grated
- 1 teaspoon olive oil
- 1 teaspoon butter

- A pinch salt
- A pinch pepper

Instructions:

1. Mix together cooked spaghetti with a little pasta sauce just enough to coat the spaghetti.
2. Add egg and cheese and mix well.
3. Place a small nonstick pan over medium heat. Add oil and butter. When butter melts, add the spaghetti mixture to it. Press well with a wooden spoon into a flat omelet. Cook until the bottom side is golden brown. Flip sides and cook the other side too.
4. Chop into wedges. Sprinkle Parmesan and serve.

Leftover Curry Pulao

Prep Time: 5 minutes

Ingredients:

- 1 cup leftover chicken or fish curry
- 3/4 cup rice, soaked in water for 15-20 minutes, drained
- A pinch salt
- 1 cup water
- 1 tablespoon cilantro leaves, chopped

Instructions:

1. Add chicken curry, soaked rice, water and salt to a saucepan.
2. Place the saucepan over medium heat. Cook until the rice is soft.
3. Garnish with cilantro and serve.

Lemon Rice

Prep Time: 5 minutes

Ingredients:

- 2 cups leftover cooked rice
- 1 medium onion, sliced thinly lengthwise
- 1/4 teaspoon turmeric
- 1 tablespoon olive oil
- 1/2 teaspoon mustard seeds
- 2 tablespoons lemon juice
- 1/2 teaspoon salt or to taste
- 2 green chilies, slit
- 8-10 curry leaves

Instructions:

1. Place a nonstick skillet over medium heat. Add oil. When oil is hot, add mustard seeds. The mustard seeds will start spluttering.
2. When the spluttering stops, add onions, curry leaves and green chilies. Sauté until the onions are translucent.
3. Add turmeric powder and sauté for a few seconds. Add salt and rice and heat thoroughly. Remove from heat.
4. Add lemon juice and mix well.

Leftover Chicken and Noodles

This is a very simple and easy leftover chicken and noodles recipe that is perfect for anyone who does not have a lot of time to cook elaborate dishes for one.

Prep time: 10 minutes

Cooking time; 30 minutes

Ingredients:

- 1/3 cup of cooked leftover chicken breast meat, diced
- 26 ounce (1/8 can) cream of chicken soup, condensed
- 11 ounce (1/8 can) cream of mushroom soup, condensed
- 14.5 ounce (1/2 can) of chicken broth
- 9 ounce of frozen egg noodles
- ¼ tsp of onion powder
- 1/8 tsp of garlic powder
- Seasoning salt to taste

Instructions:

1. Combine the cream of mushroom soup, cream of chicken soul, leftover chicken breast meat, and chicken broth in a pot. Add your seasonings including salt, onion powder, and garlic powder.
2. Bring the mixture to a boil and add the noodles.
3. Lower the heat and let simmer for 20 minutes to half an hour.

Bubble 'n' Squeak

Everything that you need is in this dish—bacon, ham, cabbage, potatoes, and onions. This is a great recipe to encourage kids to eat cabbage. This is a main dish that is so quick to make because you are using leftover potatoes.

Prep time: 15 minutes

Cooking time: 15 minutes

Ingredients:

- 1/2 cup of cooked potatoes, thinly sliced
- 1/8 medium-sized cabbage head, sliced
- 1/8 onion, sliced thinly
- ½ slice of bacon, diced
- 2 tbsp and 2 tsp of cooked ham, cubed
- ½ tsp of butter
- 1/8 tsp of paprika
- Season with salt and pepper

Instructions:

1. Pour a small amount of water in a saucepan and cook cabbage until tender, or about 5 minutes. Drain the water and set aside the cooked cabbage.
2. Use a non-stick pan and cook onion and bacon. Once onions are tender and bacon is cooked, toss in the ham. When the ham is hot enough, add the butter, cooked cabbage, and leftover potatoes. Mix well.
3. Sprinkle with salt, pepper, and paprika for a more enhanced flavour. Cook the ingredients until all sides are browned.
4. Serve with ketchup, if preferred.

Enchiladas for Brunch

These enchiladas burst with flavour because of the mixture of different ingredients which include ham, cheese, and vegetables. The use of creamy egg batter adds even more flavour to this scrumptious brunch recipe. This makes 2 servings.

Prep time: 30 minutes

Cooking time: 1 hour

Ingredients:

- 2 tortillas made of flour (7 inch)
- 1 beaten egg
- 3 ounces of ham, cooked and chopped
- ½ cup, 1 tbsp, and 2 tsp cheddar cheese, shredded and divided
- 2 tbsp and 1 ¼ tsp of green bell peppers, chopped
- 2 tbsp and 1 ¼ tsp of green onions, sliced
- 1 tbsp and 1 ¾ tsp of milk
- 1/3 cup and 1 tbsp of cream
- 1/8 tsp of garlic powder
- ½ tsp of flour
- Hot pepper sauce

Instructions:

1. Using a food processor, pulse the cooked ham until finely ground. Transfer the ground ham into a bowl and mix in green peppers and green onions.
2. Using a spoon put about 1/3 cup of this ham mixture onto each flour tortilla. Add 3 tablespoons of shredded cheddar cheese to each tortilla before rolling them up. Put the tortillas with the edges facing down to ensure that it will remain in place.
3. Put the tortillas in a greased baking sheet.
4. Combine the flour, cream, eggs, milk, hot pepper sauce, and garlic powder in a bowl. Gently pour this mixture over your tortillas. Cover the baking sheet with aluminium foil and put it in the fridge overnight.

5. When you wake up the next day, preheat oven at 350 degrees F.

6. Remove the aluminium foil cover and bake for about an hour or 50 minutes, to ensure that the enchiladas are properly set.

Egg Salad Sandwiches

Egg salad sandwiches use leftover fresh ingredients from your previous dishes.

Prep time: 10 minutes

Cooking time: 15 minutes

Ingredients:

- 2 eggs
- 1 tbsp of green onions, chopped
- 2 tbsp of mayonnaise
- ¼ tsp of yellow mustard, prepared
- 1/8 tsp of paprika
- Season with pepper and salt

Instructions:

1. Pour water in a saucepan and put the eggs, making sure that the eggs are covered with water. Boil the eggs and remove the pan from heat immediately after boiling. Cover the pan and allow the egg to sit in hot water for another 12 minutes or so. Get the eggs out of the pan and let them cool before peeling and chopping.

2. Once the eggs are chopped, put them in a bowl and add the other ingredients including mustard, mayonnaise, and green onion. Sprinkle with paprika, pepper, and salt

according to preferred taste. Stir all the ingredients together.

3. Serve with crackers or bread.

Mashed Potato Cakes

Mashed potato cakes are popular in the South. You can use leftover potatoes and other fresh ingredients to make this recipe.

Prep time: 20 minutes

Cooking time: 35 minutes

Ingredients:

- ¼ cup and 1 tbsp mashed potatoes
- ¾ slice of bacon
- 1 and ½ tsp of butter
- ¼ celery stalk, roughly chopped
- ¼ onion, chopped
- ¼ cup American cheese, shredded
- 1 slightly beaten egg (only use ¼)
- 1/8 tsp garlic, minced
- 1/8 tsp yellow mustard, prepared
- 3 tbsp flour, all-purpose
- 1 and ½ tsp sour cream
- A dash of hot sauce
- ¾ tsp vegetable oil
- 1/8 tsp freshly ground pepper or to taste

Instructions:

1. Cook bacon over medium to high heat in a large non-stick skillet. Turn the bacon occasionally to ensure even

browning on both sides. Bacon will cook for about 10 minutes. Put the slices of bacon on paper towels to drain the oil. Once the bacon slices are cooled, crumble them into smaller pieces.

2. Over medium to high heat, heat the butter to melt in the same skillet where you cooked the bacon. Toss in the celery, onion, and garlic until lightly browned and tender. This will take about 15 minutes. Put the bacon and vegetables in a large mixing bowl.

3. Stir in the mashed potatoes, flour, American cheese, egg, pepper, hot sauce, and mustard.

4. In a clean non-stick skillet, heat vegetable oil and drop about a spoonful of the mashed potato mixture onto the pan. Using the same spoon or spatula, flatten the mashed potato mixture, creating patties and then fry them until well-cooked, or when the color turns golden brown. This takes about 5 minutes or so.

5. You can serve this mashed potato cakes with sour cream.

Chapter 11: Quick 15-Minute Recipes for One

Most people who live alone find it too troublesome to prepare food for one that will require them to spend at least an hour in the kitchen. If you are too busy to prepare an elaborate meal, this chapter will help you prepare quick and easy 15-minute recipes for one.

Corn and Cheese Toasties

If you always bring lunch to work and you are running out of ideas, this is a great recipe that you can prepare in the morning and bring to work. It has cheese, mayo, and corned beef, making it not only a favorite among the singles but also among kids.

Prep time: 5 minutes

Cooking time: 10 minutes

Ingredients:

- 2 slices of bread
- 1 tsp of mayo
- 1 tbsp of butter
- 1 slice of American cheese
- 1 slice of corned beef in can

Instructions:

1. Put a skillet on the stove at medium to high heat. Get your bread slices and spread butter on one side of each bread slice. Using a spoon, spread mayo on the sides without butter.

2. Toast the bread on the skillet by placing them on the hot skillet with the buttered side facing down. While the bread slices are cooking, add a layer of corned beef and add the cheese slices on top of the bread.

3. Put the remaining halves of the bread on top with the buttered side facing upwards. Cook each side of the sandwich until the cheese melted and the color turns golden brown, or about 5 minutes.

Salmon Glazed with Brown Sugar

This is not only quick and easy but also a healthy source of protein and omega-3 oil. You can serve this with broccoli and rice. This recipe makes 2 servings.

Prep time: 5 minutes

Cooking time: 10 minutes

Ingredients:

- 2 pieces (6 ounces each) salmon fillets, boneless
- 2 tbsp of light brown sugar, packed
- 1 tbsp of Dijon mustard
- Freshly ground pepper and salt for seasoning

Instructions:

1. Preheat your oven's broiler and position the rack several inches away from the source of heat. Spray a broiler pan with cooking spray to prevent sticking.

2. Get the salmon and evenly coat all sides with pepper and salt. Put the salmon fillets on the sprayed broiler pan.

3. In a small bowl, combine the Dijon mustard and brown sugar and put the mixture on top of each salmon fillet.

4. Cook the salmon fillets for 10 minutes, or until the fish is tender and can be easily flaked off using a fork.

Eggplant Burgers

Vegetarians or people who are trying to lose weight will surely love this recipe. This veggie burger s not only easy to make, it is also budget-friendly, which makes it perfect for people who live solo. You can mix and match different types of cheeses and toppings depending on your preferences.

Prep time: 7 minutes

Cooking time: 7 minutes

Ingredients:

- 2 pieces of hamburger buns, sliced horizontally in the middle
- 1 small eggplant, peeled and sliced into rounds
- 2 lettuce leaves
- 2 tomato slices
- 2 Monterey Jack cheese slices
- About ¼ onion, sliced
- 1 tsp of margarine
- A dollop of ketchup
- About 3 tbsp of dill pickle slices
- 1 tbsp of mayo
- 2 tsp of yellow mustard, prepared

Instructions:

1. You can cook the eggplant slices in a microwave until the centers are cooked, or about 5 minutes.

2. Place a large skillet on the stove at medium to high heat and put the margarine to melt. Toast the egg plant slices on both sides. Top the eggplant slices with cheese and cook until the cheese has already melted before removing the eggplants from the skillet.

3. Get your hamburger buns and place your eggplant and cheese slices. Top with the remaining ingredients, depending on what you like your burger to have. Add mustard, mayo, and ketchup.

Fettuccine with Cayenne and Sweet Pepper Sauce

This is dish full of flavour because of the variety of ingredients. To turn it into an even more wonderful dish, you can add shredded grilled chicken. It is a healthy recipe that can serve two people.

Prep time: 5 minutes

Cooking time: 10 minutes

Ingredients:

- 6 ounces of fettuccine pasta, preferably dry
- A quarter tsp of cayenne pepper
- 1 medium-sized red bell pepper, julienned
- Half a cup of sour cream, reduced-fat
- About 2 cloves of garlic, minced
- About ¼ cup of parmesan cheese, grated
- About ¼ cup of chicken broth
- Pepper and salt for seasoning

Instructions:

1. Pour water in a pot and add a dash of salt. Boil water. Add your fettuccine pasta into the pot and cook until al dente, which takes about 8 to 10 minutes. Drain the pasta and set aside.

2. While pasta is cooking, prepare a skillet by lightly coating it with cooking spray. Sauté your garlic, red bell peppers and cayenne pepper on the skillet for about 3 to 5 minutes over medium heat.

3. Pour the broth and sour cream into the skillet. Let it simmer for about 5 minutes without cover. Remove the skillet from the heat source and mix in the cheese. This will be your sauce.

4. Stir in the hot fettuccine pasta with the sauce. Add pepper and salt to taste. Serve while still hot.

These are all great recipes that can serve one or two people. These recipes are perfect for those people who want to eat home-cooked meals even though they live by themselves. It is important that you still make an effort even if you do not have anyone to cook for aside from yourself because eating home-cooked meals is not only good for your health but also for your budget.

Chapter 12: Smoothies for One

Strawberry and Banana Smoothie:

Prep Time: 5 minutes

Ingredients:

- 1 small banana, sliced
- 1/2 cup frozen strawberries
- 1/3 cup nonfat milk
- 1/2 cup low fat strawberry flavored yogurt

Instructions:

1. Blend together all the ingredients in a blender until smooth.
2. Pour in a tall glass and serve with crushed ice.

Chocolate Hemp Smoothie

Prep Time: 5 minutes

Ingredients:

- 1 large medjool date, soaked in water for a couple of hours
- 1 cup almond milk
- 1 1/2 tablespoons unsweetened cocoa powder
- 1 1/2 tablespoon hemp seeds, hulled
- 1 medium frozen banana
- A large pinch ground cinnamon

Instructions:

1. Blend together all the ingredients in a blender until smooth.
2. Pour in a tall glass and serve with crushed ice.

Tropical Smoothie

Prep Time: 10 minutes

Instructions:

- 1 cup coconut water
- 1/2 cup coconut, chopped into pieces
- 2 slices pineapple, chopped into pieces
- 1 kiwi fruit, peeled, chopped into pieces

Instructions:

1. Blend together all the ingredients in a blender until smooth.
2. Pour in a tall glass and serve with crushed ice.

Apricot Smoothie:

Prep Time: 5 minutes

Ingredients:

- 1 cup apricots, pitted, chopped
- 1/2 cup plain yogurt
- Sweetener of your choice
- 1 cup romaine lettuce, torn
- 1 small banana, peeled, chopped
- Blend together all the ingredients in a blender until smooth.

- Pour in a tall glass and serve with crushed ice.

Instructions:

1. Blend together all the ingredients in a blender until smooth.
2. Pour in a tall glass and serve with crushed ice.

Berry Blast

Ingredients:

- 1 cup mixed berries of your choice
- 1 cup water
- 1 cup mango, chopped

Instructions:

1. Blend together all the ingredients in a blender until smooth.
2. Pour in a tall glass and serve with crushed ice.

Antioxidant Smoothie

Prep Time: 10 minutes

Ingredients:

- 1 cup spinach
- 1 cup kale
- 1 cups papaya, cubed
- 1 banana, sliced
- 1 green apple, cored, chopped
- 1/2 cup water

Instructions:

1. Blend together all the ingredients in a blender until smooth.
2. Pour in a tall glass and serve with crushed ice.

Chocolate Dates Smoothie

Prep Time: 5 minutes

Ingredients:

- 2 large dates, pitted, soaked in water for a while if it is hard, chopped
- 1 1/2 cups almond milk
- 1 tablespoon hemp seeds, hulled
- 1 tablespoon unsweetened cocoa powder
- 1/8teaspoon ground cinnamon
- 1 small banana, chopped

Instructions:

1. Blend together all the ingredients in a blender until smooth.
2. Pour in a tall glass and serve with crushed ice.

Chapter 13: Drinks and Beverages for One

Frozen Mojito

Prep time: 15 minutes

Ingredients:

- 2 tablespoons sugar syrup (1 tablespoon water boiled with 1 tablespoon sugar)
- Juice of a lime
- 2 ounces white rum
- A few mint leaves
- 1/2 cup crushed ice
- A couple of sprigs of mint for garnishing

Instructions:

1. Blend together sugar syrup, lime juice and mint leaves.
2. Add rum and ice and blend again until frothy.
3. Pour into a glass and garnish with sprigs of mint.

Iced Mocha

Prep time: 5 minutes

Ingredients:

- 1 cup strong brewed coffee, chilled
- 1 teaspoon brown sugar

- 1 teaspoon chocolate sauce
- 3/4 cup chocolate milk

Instructions:

1. Blend together all the ingredients until frothy.
2. Pour into a tall glass. Add ice cubes and serve.

Fresh Berry Limeade

Prep Time: 5 minutes

Ingredients:

- 1/4 cup strawberries, chopped
- 2 tablespoons raspberries
- 1 teaspoon agave nectar or any sweetener of your choice
- 2 tablespoons lime juice
- 3/4 cup club soda or as required

Instructions:

1. Blend together all the ingredients except soda until frothy.
2. Pour into a tall glass. Add soda as much as you require. Add ice cubes and serve.

Watermelon Juice

Prep Time: 5 minutes

Ingredients:

- 1 cup watermelon, deseeded, cubed
- 1/2 cup water
- Juice of 1/2 a lime

- 1/8 teaspoon black salt (optional)

Instructions:

1. Blend together all the ingredients until smooth.
2. Pour into a tall glass. Add ice cubes and serve.

Blueberry Rum Milkshake

Prep Time: 10 minutes

Ingredients:

- 1/2 cup blueberries
- 2 tablespoons dark rum
- 2 tablespoons sugar
- 1/2 teaspoon vanilla extract
- 3/4 cup vanilla ice cream
- 3 tablespoons milk
- A few blueberries to garnish

Instructions:

1. Blend together all the ingredients until smooth.
2. Pour into a tall glass. Add crushed ice. Garnish with a few blueberries and serve.

Fruit Punch

Prep Time: 10 minutes

Ingredients:

- 1/2 cup apple juice
- 1/2 cup orange juice
- 1 tablespoon lemon juice

- 1/2 teaspoon ginger, finely grated
- 2 tablespoons apple, grated
- A little club soda

Instructions:

1. Mix together all the ingredients except soda. Chill in the refrigerator.
2. Pour into a tall glass. Fill up with club soda and serve with crushed ice

Chapter 14: Salads for One

For whisking the dressing: Add all the ingredients of the dressing to a small jar with a tightly screwed lid. Shake thoroughly.

Sweetheart Slaw:

Prep Time: 10 minutes

Ingredients:

- 3/4 cup red cabbage, shredded
- 3 tablespoons red bell pepper, chopped
- 2 strawberries, sliced
- 1/4 cup mango, peeled, chopped
- 1 tablespoon olive oil
- 1 tablespoon honey
- 1 1/2 tablespoons balsamic vinegar

Instructions:

1. Add all the ingredients to a bowl and toss well. Chill for a while before serving.

Apple Chicken Salad

Prep Time: 10 minutes + chilling time

Ingredients:

- 1 small apple, chopped
- 1 cup chicken, chopped into bite sized pieces, cubed
- 1 cup lettuce leaves, torn into bite sized pieces
- 2 tablespoons yellow bell pepper, chopped

- 2 tablespoon green bell pepper, chopped
- 1/4 cup mayonnaise
- 1 teaspoon pimentos, chopped
- Salt to taste
- Pepper powder to taste

Instructions:

1. Add all the ingredients except lettuce and toss well. Refrigerate until chilled.
2. Add lettuce, mix well and serve.

Asian Sprout Salad with Carrots

Prep Time: 25 minutes

Ingredients:

- 1/2 cup bean sprouts
- 1 small cucumber, make ribbons using a vegetable peeler
- 1 medium carrot, make ribbons using a vegetable peeler
- 1/4 cup snow peas, thinly sliced
- 2 tablespoons snow peas sprouts, trimmed
- 1 teaspoon sesame seeds, toasted

For Dressing:
- 1/2 teaspoon sesame oil
- 1/2 tablespoon olive oil
- 1/2 teaspoon honey
- 1/2 tablespoon rice wine vinegar

Instructions:

1. To make dressing: Whisk together all the ingredients of the dressing.
2. Place carrots and snow peas in a heatproof bowl. Pour boiling hot over it.
3. Cover and keep aside for a couple of minutes. Drain and rinse under cold water. Drain thoroughly and transfer to a bowl.
4. Add rest of the ingredients. Pour dressing. Toss well and serve.

Avocado & Beetroot Salad

Prep Time: 15 minutes

Ingredients:

- 1 medium beetroot, peeled, thinly sliced
- 1/4 cup red wine vinegar
- 1 teaspoon extra virgin olive oil
- 1 avocado, peeled, pitted, thinly sliced

For Dressing:
- 1/2 tablespoon white vinegar
- 1 teaspoon lemon juice
- 2-3 segments mandarin orange
- 3 tablespoons extra virgin olive oil
- 1 tablespoon orange juice
- A pinch of sugar
- A pinch of salt
- A pinch of pepper powder
- 1 teaspoon chervil, chopped

- 1 tablespoon spring onions, chopped

Instructions:

1. To make the dressing: Mix together in a bowl, vinegar, spring onions, salt, lemon juice and orange juice and keep aside for 10 minutes. Gently whisk olive oil and keep aside.
2. Place orange segments in a mortar and pestle. Do not remove the skin. Add sugar and pound to a rough paste.
3. Add the orange paste and chervil to the oil mixture. Add salt and pepper.
4. Meanwhile, place the beetroot slices on a lined baking tray. Sprinkle olive oil and red wine vinegar over it. Cover and set aside for 10 minutes.
5. Drain the beetroots and rinse in cold water.
6. Lay the beetroot slices on a serving plate. Lay the avocado slices over the beetroot slices. Sprinkle salt and pepper.
7. Pour the dressing on top and serve garnished with a few sprigs of chervil.

Greek Chicken Salad

Prep Time: 25 minutes

Ingredients:

- 1 1/2 cups romaine lettuce
- 3/4 cup chicken, chopped, cooked
- 1 small tomato, chopped
- 1/4 cup cucumber, peeled, seeded, chopped
- 2 tablespoons feta cheese, crumbled

- 2 tablespoons ripe black olives, chopped
- 2 tablespoons red onions, finely chopped

For the Dressing:

- 1/2 tablespoon extra virgin olive oil
- A pinch salt
- A pinch pepper powder
- 1/4 teaspoon garlic powder
- 1 1/4 tablespoons red wine vinegar
- 1/4 teaspoon dried oregano

Instructions:

1. To make the dressing: Whisk together all the ingredients of the dressing.
2. Add all the salad ingredients except feta cheese to a bowl. Pour dressing. Toss well and serve garnished with feta cheese.

Chicken Caesar Salad

Prep Time: 15 minutes

Ingredients:

- 1 1/2 cups romaine lettuce, chopped
- 1/2 cup skinless, boneless, cooked chicken breasts
- 1 slice multi grain bread, chopped into cubes
- 1/4 cup cucumbers, chopped
- 1/4 cup cherry tomatoes, halved
- 1/4 teaspoon dried oregano
- 2 tablespoons creamy Caesar dressing

- 1 tablespoon parmesan cheese
- Cooking spray

Instructions:

1. Spray a baking sheet with cooking spray. Place the bread cubes over it. Spray some more cooking spray over it. Sprinkle oregano.
2. Bake in a preheated oven at 350 degree F for about 10 minutes or until crisp.
3. Add all the ingredients to a bowl. Toss well. Top with croutons and serve.

Mexican Salad

Prep Time: 10 minutes

Ingredients:

- 1 large flour tortilla, cut into crouton sized pieces
- 1/2 tablespoon olive oil
- 1/2 iceberg lettuce, shredded
- 6-8 cherry tomatoes, halved
- 1 cup canned black beans, rinsed, drained
- 1 avocado, peeled, pitted, sliced
- 1/4 cup cilantro leaves, chopped
- 1/2 teaspoon Mexican seasoning

For dressing:

- Juice of a lime
- 1 tablespoon extra virgin olive oil
- 1/4 teaspoon Tabasco sauce
- 1/8 teaspoon salt
- 1/8 teaspoon pepper to taste

Instructions:

1. Mix together all the ingredients of the dressing and keep aside.
2. Place the tortilla pieces on a baking sheet. Add oil and toss it well. Sprinkle seasoning.
3. Bake in a preheated oven at 350 degree F until crisp.
4. Add all the salad ingredients to a bowl and toss well.

5. Pour the dressing over it. Toss well. Garnish with coriander leaves and top with croutons and serve.

Chapter 15: Simmering Soup Recipes

Broccoli Cheese Soup

Prep Time: 15 minutes

Ingredients:

- 2 tablespoons onions, chopped
- 1/2 cup vegetable broth or chicken broth
- 1 clove garlic, minced
- 1/2 tablespoon all purpose flour
- 1 cup fresh broccoli florets
- 1/2 cup milk
- 1/8 teaspoon dried tarragon
- 1/8 teaspoon dried thyme
- 1/3 cup cheddar cheese, shredded
- A pinch pepper powder
- A pinch salt
- Cooking spray

Instructions:

1. Place a nonstick pan over medium heat. Spray with cooking spray. Add onions and garlic and sauté until tender.
2. Add flour and sauté for a few seconds. Add broth and stir constantly until it thickens.
3. Add broccoli, tarragon, thyme, salt and pepper and bring to a boil.

4. Lower heat, cover and simmer until broccoli is tender. Add milk cook uncovered for 5 minutes.

5. Remove from heat. Cool it for about 10 minutes. Blend in a blender until smooth.

6. Reheat the soup adding half the cheese. Heat until the cheese is melted and well blended in the soup.

7. Pour into a soup bowl. Garnish with the remaining cheese. Serve immediately.

Chicken Noodle Soup

Prep Time: 10 minutes

Ingredients:

- 2 tablespoons onions, chopped
- 1/2 cup skinless, boneless, chicken breast cubes
- 1 can (14 1/2 ounces) chicken broth
- 1 clove garlic, minced
- 1 tablespoon olive oil
- 1/2 tablespoon butter
- 1 small carrot, peeled, sliced
- 2 tablespoons frozen peas, thawed
- 1/4 teaspoon dried basil
- 1 cup uncooked egg noodles
- 1 tablespoon lemon juice

Instructions:

1. Place a saucepan over medium heat. Add oil and butter. When butter melts, add chicken and sauté until chicken is light brown.

2. Add garlic and sauté until fragrant (approximately a minute)

3. Add broth, carrots, peas and basil and bring to a boil.

4. Lower heat, cover and simmer for 5 minutes. Add noodles. Cover and cook until the noodles are al dente. If the soup is too thick you can add some water to dilute it. Add lemon juice and mix well.

5. Ladle into a soup bowl and serve hot.

Couscous Paella Soup

Prep time: 15 minutes

Ingredients:

- 2 tablespoons Spanish chorizo, finely diced
- 2 ounces chicken tenders, cut into 1/2 inch pieces
- 1 cup chicken broth
- 1 teaspoon extra virgin olive oil
- 2 tablespoons red bell pepper, diced
- 1 clove garlic, minced
- 2 tablespoons onions, diced
- 2 tablespoons frozen peas, thawed
- A pinch saffron soaked in a tablespoon of hot water
- 3 tablespoons whole wheat couscous
- 1/4 cup water
- A pinch salt
- A pinch pepper powder
- 1 tablespoon cilantro, chopped

Instructions:

1. Place a medium saucepan over medium heat. Add oil. When oil is hot, add bell pepper, chorizo, garlic, and onion. Sauté until onions are translucent.
2. Add chicken, broth, peas, salt, pepper, and saffron. Bring to a boil.
3. Lower heat, simmer until chicken is cooked.
4. Meanwhile boil water in a small saucepan. Add couscous. Cover with a lid and remove from heat. Keep aside for 5 minutes.
5. Place the couscous to a wide shallow bowl. Pour the soup all around the couscous.
6. Garnish with cilantro and serve.

French Onion Soup

Prep Time: 10 minutes

Ingredients:

- 1 small onion, sliced
- 1 teaspoon oil
- 1/2 teaspoon garlic, chopped
- 1 green onion, white and light green parts only, chopped
- 1/2 teaspoon fresh thyme, chopped
- 1/2 tablespoon sherry
- 7 ounces low sodium beef broth or vegetable broth
- 4 ounces canned chickpeas, rinsed
- 3 tablespoons fontina or Gruyere cheese, shredded
- 1 tablespoon fresh chives, minced
- Greens of the green onion, finely chopped
- 1 slice whole wheat bread, toasted

- Freshly ground black pepper to taste
- Salt to taste

Instructions:

1. Place a saucepan over medium heat. Add oil. When oil is hot, add onion. Sauté until the onions are light brown. Add leek, garlic and thyme. Sauté until the leeks become soft.
2. Add sherry and pepper. Raise the heat to medium high and cook until the moisture almost dries up.
3. Add broth and chickpeas. Bring to a boil.
4. Lower heat and simmer until the vegetables are tender.
5. Remove from heat and add salt, chives and onion greens. Mix well.
6. Place bread in a soup bowl. Add cheese.
7. Ladle soup into the bowl and serve immediately.

Spinach and Pasta Soup

Ingredients:

- 3 tablespoons uncooked orzo
- 1 green onion, thinly sliced
- 1 clove garlic, thinly sliced
- 1 teaspoon olive oil
- 1 cup vegetable or chicken broth
- 1/2 cup water
- 3 1/2 ounces canned chickpeas, drained
- 1/2 teaspoon lemon zest, grated
- 1 teaspoon fresh oregano, chopped
- 1 teaspoon lemon juice

- A pinch salt
- A pinch black pepper powder
- 2 ounces fresh baby spinach
- 1 tablespoon grated parmesan cheese

Instructions:

1. Place a saucepan over high heat. Add olive oil. When oil is hot, add garlic and onions. Sauté for about a minute. Add broth and water and bring to a boil.
2. Add orzo, lemon zest and chickpeas. Cover and cook until orzo is tender.
3. Add rest of the ingredients and heat thoroughly.
4. Ladle into a soup bowl and serve immediately.

Chapter 16: Quick 15-Minute Recipes for One

Green Tortilla Pizza

Prep Time: 7-8 minutes

Ingredients:

- 1 whole wheat tortilla
- 2-3 tablespoons pizza sauce
- 2 button mushrooms, sliced
- 1 tablespoon onion, sliced
- 1 tablespoon bell pepper, sliced
- 2-3 tablespoons mozzarella, shredded
- 1/4 teaspoon oregano
- A pinch salt
- A pinch red chili flakes

Instructions:

1. Preheat a broiler.
2. Meanwhile chop the vegetables.
3. Place the tortilla on a lined baking sheet.
4. Spread pizza sauce over the tortilla. Sprinkle the vegetables over the tortilla.
5. Sprinkle oregano, salt and chili flakes. Finally sprinkle cheese.
6. Broil for about 4 minutes until cheese is light brown.

Banana Pancake

Prep Time: 5 minutes

Ingredients:

- 2 ripe bananas, peeled, sliced
- 1 large egg
- 2 tablespoons almond butter
- A large pinch ground cinnamon
- 1 tablespoon vegetable oil

Instructions:

1. Add all the ingredients to a blender and blend until smooth.
2. Place a nonstick pan over medium heat. Add half the oil. Swirl the pan to coat the pan with oil.
3. Pour about half the batter. Slightly swirl the pan to spread a little. Cook until the bottom side is golden brown.
4. Flip sides and cook the other side too.
5. Add the remaining oil and repeat steps 3 and 4.
6. Serve immediately.

Californian Wrap:

Prep Time: 5 minutes

Ingredients:

- 1 flour tortilla
- 2 slices cooked bacon
- 1/4 cucumber, chopped into matchsticks
- 2 ounces low fat cream cheese

- Salt to taste
- Pepper powder to taste
- 1/2 avocado, pitted, sliced

Instructions:

1. Place tortilla on serving plate. Spread the cream cheese over it.
2. Place bacon, avocado and cucumber over it. Season with salt and pepper.
3. Roll and serve.

Kale and Cauliflower Pasta

Prep Time: 5 minutes

Ingredients:

- 1/2 cup angel hair pasta
- 1/2 cup cauliflower florets
- 1 small shallot, chopped
- 1 clove garlic minced
- 1 teaspoon olive oil
- 1/2 bunch kale leaves, remove the hard stems, torn
- 2 tablespoons parmesan, grated

Instructions:

1. Place a small pot of water, covered with a lid over medium high heat. Add angel hair pasta and cauliflower florets. Bring to a boil.
2. After 2-3 minutes, remove only the cauliflower florets from the pot. Cook the pasta until al dente. Drain and retain about 1/4 cup of the boiled liquid.

3. Meanwhile place a frying pan over medium high heat. Add olive oil. When oil is hot, add shallot and garlic. Sauté for a couple of minutes.

4. Add kale. Mix well, cover and cook for 3-4 minutes until kale wilts.

5. Add pasta, Parmesan and the retained liquid. Mix well. Heat thoroughly and serve.

All in one salad

Prep time: 10 minutes

Ingredients:

- 2 cups greens of your choice
- 1 cup cooked chicken or turkey or any other meat or hardboiled egg
- 1 small tomato, chopped
- 1/4 zucchini, thinly sliced
- 2 tablespoons red bell pepper
- 2 tablespoons green bell pepper
- 1 tablespoon fresh herbs of your choice, chopped
- Dressing of your choice

Instructions:

1. Add all the ingredients to a large bowl. Toss well and serve.

Salad Layonnaise

Prep Time: 5 minutes

Ingredients:

- 1 small head chicory or Belgian endive, torn into small pieces
- 1/2 tablespoon shallot, minced
- 1 clove garlic, smashed
- 1/2 tablespoon olive oil
- 1/2 teaspoon Dijon mustard
- 2 slices bacon, cut into 1/4 inch strips
- Salt to taste
- Pepper powder to taste
- 1 tablespoon red wine
- 2 eggs, poached
- 2 slices white crustless bread, cubed

Instructions:

1. Place a nonstick skillet over medium heat. Add garlic and bacon strips and cook until bacon is crisp. Remove the bacon with a slotted spoon and set aside.
2. To the same pan, add the bread cubes and fry until crisp. Remove and keep aside.
3. Add shallots to the pan along with olive oil and sauté for a minute. Add mustard and vinegar. Mix well and remove from heat and keep aside to cool.
4. Place endive to a large bowl. Pour the dressing over it. Place the bacon over it. Top with bread croutons over the bacon and finally top with poached eggs.
5. Serve immediately.

Chapter 17: Mason jar Meals for One

When you are all alone and don't feel like cooking every day, you can spend half a weekend to prepare your meals and store it in Masons jars. All you need to do is grab a jar and a spoon and carry your own homemade delicious meal.

Pasta Salad

Prep Time: 15 minutes

Ingredients:

- 1 cup rigatoni pasta, cooked according to the instructions on the package, drained
- 1/2 cup cherry tomatoes, halved
- 1/2 cup cucumber, peeled, chopped
- 1/2 cup feta cheese, crumbled
- 1/4 cup lettuce leaves, torn
- 1/4 cup parsley leaves
- 1/4 cup fresh basil leaves
- 2-3 tablespoons basil pesto

Instructions:

1. Mix together all the ingredients in a large bowl.
2. Fill in 2 mason jars.
3. Tightly screw the lids. Refrigerate until use.
4. Can store up to 3 days.

Chick peas Salad

Prep Time: 15 minutes

Ingredients:

- 1 cup chickpeas, boiled
- 1/2 cup tomatoes, chopped
- 1/4 cup onion, chopped
- 1/4 cup olives, chopped
- 1/2 cup sweet red bell pepper, chopped
- 1 cup fresh spinach, shredded
- 1/2 cup spring onions, chopped
- 1/2 cup corn kernels

For the dressing:
- Juice of 1 lemon
- 1 small clove garlic, finely minced
- 1/4 cup extra virgin olive oil
- Salt to taste
- Pepper to taste

Instructions:

1. Mix together all the ingredients of the dressing. Whisk well.
2. Layer in the jar as follows: Pour the salad dressing right at the bottom or 2 jars
3. Next add the chickpeas followed by tomatoes, spring onions and onions.
4. Next lay the bell peppers, corn and finally the spinach.
5. Tightly screw on the lids of the jar. Refrigerate until use.
6. Toss the salad well before eating.

Granola Parfait

Prep Time: 10 minutes

Ingredients:

- 1 cup fruits of your choice
- 1 cup berries of your choice
- 1/2 cup rolled oats
- 2 tablespoons almonds, chopped
- 2 tablespoons raisins
- 1 1/2 cups plain, low fat yogurt
- 2-3 tablespoons honey or to taste
- 1/4 teaspoon ground cinnamon
- 1 teaspoon olive oil
- 1/4 teaspoon vanilla extract
- A pinch salt

Instructions:

1. Mix together in a bowl the oats, almonds, olive oil, cinnamon, vanilla, salt and 2 tablespoons honey.
2. Spread evenly on a greased baking dish.
3. Bake in a preheated oven at 350 degree F for around 45 minutes or until golden brown. Stir it 2-3 times in between.
4. To arrange in the mason jars, first fill in the yogurt, drizzle the remaining honey over it.
5. Next layer it with fruits followed by berries and then granola.
6. Tightly screw on the lids and refrigerate.
7. It can store up to 3 days.

Eggs and Bacon in a Masons jar

Prep Time: 5-7 minutes

Ingredients:

- 3 eggs
- 3/4 cup spinach, finely shredded
- 1/2 cup cheese,
- 1/4 cup bacon, crumbled
- Salt to taste
- Pepper powder to taste

Instructions:

1. Mix together the eggs, spinach, cheese, salt and pepper.
2. Fill this in 2 Masons jars.
3. Microwave for 1 1/2 to 2 minutes.
4. As it is being micro waved, the egg will rise to the top of the jar. Not to worry.
5. Top with bacon and extra cheese if you if you are a cheese lover.
6. Tightly screw the lids on the jars
7. Store in the refrigerator.
8. Can store for 2-3 days

Overnight Apple Pie Oatmeal

Ingredients:

- 1 1/2 cups soy milk or almond milk (plain or flavored, your choice)
- 1/4 cup plain yogurt
- ½ cup oatmeal
- 1 tablespoon maple syrup or honey
- 1/2 cup apples, chopped
- 1/2 teaspoon ground cinnamon

Instructions:

1. Mix together all the ingredients well.
2. Fill up 2 Masons Jars with it.
3. Refrigerate until use.
4. Can store for 3 days.

Printed in Great Britain
by Amazon